By an Unfamiliar Path

By an Unfamiliar Path

THE STORY OF
DAVID AND ARLENE PETERS

David and Arlene Peters

Christian Publications
CAMP HILL, PENNSYLVANIA

Christian Publications, Inc.
3825 Hartzdale Drive
Camp Hill, PA 17011
www.cpi-horizon.com
www.christianpublications.com

Faithful, biblical publishing since 1883

By an Unfamiliar Path
ISBN: 0-87509-580-1

LOC Catalog Card Number: 94-69126

© 1994 by Christian Publications, Inc.

00   01   02   03   04   6   5   4   3   2

Cover illustration © 1994 by Karl Foster

Contents

*We dedicate this book to our children
Kurt and Karla
whose lives have brought us incredible
joy and blessing
and whose obedience to the Lord
has been our greatest reward.*

Foreword

As we were leaving Colombia in 1971 after 10 years of ministry, David and Arlene Peters were arriving.

Dave was quiet, with a unique sense of humor. Arlene came across as a disciplined, nurse-type. Since those initial impressions in the early 70s I have discovered much more.

Behind Dave's quiet, unassuming exterior is a dogged determination to strategize for success and an ability to read people and situations. He once told me: "Missionaries who have worked in multiple staffs in North America fit in best in Latin America. They know how to work with national church leaders."

Arlene, the trained professional, quickly became an effective teacher, writer and godly counselor. I've often challenged such young people with this advice: "God may choose to use you in your field of training but it's also His prerogative to ask you to retool for another ministry. He takes fishermen and makes them apostles." Arlene allowed God to retool her.

Redeployment of experienced missionaries into new areas is a mission society's greatest and most difficult challenge at the end of the 20th century. Just when workers are getting comfortable and seeing results, there can be a new and unfamiliar path facing them.

It's a hard call, but the Peters rose to the challenge, transferring from Colombia to Brazil in 1986 and learning yet another language.

Unfamiliar paths are tough on a family—unless parents can effectively communicate their missionary passion to their children. Dave and Arlene managed to do that. Their children, Karla and Kurt, are dynamic testimonies to how God honors parents who model commitment to Him, their family and the missionary mandate—in that order.

Dr. Arnold Cook
President, The Christian and
Missionary Alliance in Canada
May, 1994

Preface

*"I will lead the blind by ways they have not
known, along unfamiliar paths I will guide
them" (Isaiah 42:16).*

L
ike most people, Arlene and I prefer comfort
to discomfort, pleasure to pain. We do not
normally choose unfamiliar paths. We are
generally more at ease with what is familiar to us,
with what we can control.

For example, once every week here in São Paulo,
our path leads us to the same restaurant. We always go on the same day, order the same thing
(pizza) and it always tastes exactly the same. We're
comfortable with that.

An unfamiliar path represents lack of control, uncertainty, possible pain and, with my poor sense of
direction, the prospect of getting hopelessly lost.

It can, however, be a path that provides fulfillment, an opportunity to grow and the joy of discovery.

Our story is one of unfamiliar paths, of God
moving us time after time out of our comfort zone
and into an obscure unknown.

It begins in Canada, then moves to Costa Rica,
Colombia and Brazil. It covers a range of ministries
from tribal work in the Andes Mountains to church

planting in a city of 18 million people.

It has been an exciting adventure, often painful, but never boring. Our prayer is that as we share our lives with you, you will be encouraged to move out of your own comfort zone and experience the joy of heading down an unfamiliar path, hand in hand with God.

David Peters
January 1994

✦ ✦ ✦

"If there's one thing I'll never be, it's a missionary!"

In my view, missionaries most always appeared outdated, haggard and unhappy as they took their places at the guest tables in the dining hall at Caronport High School.

When they spoke in chapel they looked like the last remnant of a defeated army. Although I'm sure it was there, I never really heard the cry of victory they must have brought. I just knew that the last thing in the world I wanted to be was a missionary if that's what it did to people.

However, during my senior year of high school, that negative vision was challenged and changed by the life of a vivacious young missionary widow whose husband had been killed in an accident in France during their language study year.

Childless, she had returned to Canada and to Caronport. She taught the Sunday School class I attended. Her life communicated peace and joy. Through her fragrance I realized that my mental picture of missionaries was not the reality of a life sold out to Christ and to His service.

During that year, God called me to be a missionary.

I love being a missionary.

It's not that I live from glory to glory without struggles and defeat or that I automatically enjoy everything that missionary life involves.

The delight in missionary service comes from the continual oportunities to be a first-hand witness to the working of God, of being on the front lines of battle, of experiencing that emotional rush of plunging in with the assurance that the risks have already been taken care of by Christ and victory is sure.

There's delight in knowing that even though the way the Lord leads us is unknown and unfamiliar to us, it is not to Him. He knows well the dangers and pitfalls that await us, as well as the opportunities that He has ordained.

He provides the rest stops for spiritual or physical refreshing at just the right time and He *always* leads us down paths that are good for us.

Arlene Peters
January 1994

1

Unfamiliar Paths

(Arlene)

Lying awake beside Karla's bassinette listening to her breathe, I expected each ragged gasp to be her last. Our five-week-old baby was dying and there was nothing we could do but wait in the darkness and pray that she would live until daybreak.

My pregnancy had been a difficult one. We were continually confronted with the possibility of losing our second child. We had been living in the city of Ibague, Colombia for only a few months, but already felt as if we were "real" missionaries.

Ibague was a city of 200,000 nestled in a valley high in the Andes mountains. While it was not an uncomfortable place to live, it didn't have many of the facilities that a bigger city could offer, especially medical facilities.

The Lord had provided a good doctor and with his care my pregnancy came to term. Karla was born in the Clinica Marly on March 13, 1971 without complications. The nurses placed her in a bassinette at my bedside. I thought I would burst with love for her and gratitude to God. It was such a relief that things had turned out well.

Three-year-old Kurt and Dave were with us as I gave her her first bath that day. I peeled the little bonnet off her unwashed head, removing some of the few hairs she had. The nurse didn't know I was bathing her. Colombians believe that it is harmful to a baby to be bathed before it is three days old. Precious body heat can be lost, they think.

She was a perfect, robust infant weighing over nine pounds and patients and visitors in the hospital came to greet us and to see this little North American wonder. Kurt was so proud and possessive of her, protesting fiercely when the Colombians teased him with, "Me la regala? (Will you give her to me?)"

How we enjoyed that first month of her life—until one afternoon when she was five weeks old she began to have explosive diarrhea. When the diarrhea turned bloody about two hours later I knew she was in trouble.

We bundled her up, walked to the corner and caught a taxi to the doctor's office. He examined her and ordered some tests but couldn't find anything that defined the problem.

We took her home with instructions to observe her and to give her lots of liquids. She took small amounts of formula but as soon as she drank, the diarrhea would start almost immediately.

The next morning she was listless, not drinking well and her abdomen was distended. We took her back to the doctor. He explained that the tests indicated the problem was not infectious, but he still had no inkling of a diagnosis.

He didn't want to put her in the hospital because the risk of infection there was high, and in her weakened condition, that could be fatal. Having been in that hospital for three days, I, too, believed that she was better off at home. So we bundled her up and took a taxi back home. Our only recourse now was prayer.

The situation worsened. The swelling of her little body increased until she couldn't open her eyes and she took only sips of the liquids I tried to give her.

Dave and I were in continual prayer and, as we prayed and talked and waited, the Lord impressed on Dave that this was an occasion not just for praying but for fasting. I had never fasted before but was certainly ready to now. So we began to fast and pray that God's perfect will would be done in this situation.

We were totally helpless. I was a nurse but I couldn't help my baby. The doctor was baffled. Karla's condition was deteriorating. Suddenly the excitement of living in a foreign country turned to fear. How I longed to be back in Canada surrounded by familiar faces, modern hospitals and doctors that spoke English!

That night the swelling continued to increase and the diarrhea did not abate. Karla's throat was so swollen that each breath was an effort. I stayed by her, willing her strength to take each new breath.

As I lay there in the darkness, I came face to face with the fact that the Lord could take our baby to be with Him. In fact, it looked more than probable.

Here we were, new missionaries who had "sacrificed all" to serve the Lord in this mountain city. Excerpts from many missionary biographies and stories I had read came to mind. We would not be the first missionaries to lose a child on the field.

In the silence of those moments, I placed Karla on the altar, trusting God to do what was right and good for us whether in death or in life. I wept, but I was at peace.

Morning dawned and Karla was still with us. We continued to fast and pray and once again we bundled her up, caught the taxi and made the trip to the doctor's office. When he saw us, he grinned from ear to ear. We could hardly understand the rapid Spanish that exploded from his mouth.

In his hand was an American medical journal he had just received in the mail. He pointed to an article and exclaimed, "This is your baby's problem!" The title of the article was "Milk Intolerances in Newborns."

In God's perfect timing that journal had arrived with hope and answers that would save Karla's life.

Coincidence? No. God was far ahead of us in our walk down this unfamiliar path of total commitment. He had everything worked out even before we had a need.

Within a few hours of initiating the new treatment, Karla was better.

There would be many more unfamiliar paths to walk and, if we were to see God at work, we needed to learn to trust Him completely.

2

Living on the Edge

(Arlene)

For as long as I could remember I always wanted to live on the cutting edge of life. I wanted to see what there was to see, feel what there was to feel, experience all that there was to experience. Somehow there always seemed to be something more out there beyond the normal boundaries of my life chipping away at any sense of permanence.

During my last year at Caronport High, perched on the Saskatchewan prairies, a missionary film was shown in the chapel. The film ended with the missionary's premature death and the question, "Who will go and finish the task?"

The Lord seemed to be directing the question at me and silently I responded that I would go. From that time on, I knew that I would one day be a missionary.

I had accepted Christ at Ness Lake Bible Camp when I was 13. Though my parents weren't Christians, they were happy with my decision. Having a teenager that always wanted to live on the edge was becoming a bit nerve-wracking and they were glad for anything that might change the direction of my life.

The first week back from camp I looked up the nearest church as I had been counseled to do. I made an appointment to talk with the pastor and met him in his office.

"I've just been saved at Bible camp," I explained, "and I need to know what to do now."

He thought for a moment, then said, "Well, just live according to your conscience."

Unfortunately, my former life had not produced a conscience that could be trusted. So the next two years were the worst of my life. How different they could have been if only I had had someone to disciple me into a walk with the Lord.

Relationships with my parents continued to deteriorate. Lying to keep out of trouble became such a normal part of life that I sometimes had difficulty differentiating between the truth and the fiction that I invented. I did everything I could to be a part of what was known as the "wrong crowd."

In spite of all my efforts, this life that I wanted to live to the full was full of pain and unhappiness. There were days when it seemed that the logical thing to do would be to throw myself in front of a passing truck and put an end to it.

When I was 15 my parents realized that to save anything good left in me I needed to get out of Prince George, a frontier-like town known for its on-the-edge lifestyle. They had heard about a resident high school that had a good record of helping young people with problems. I'm sure it was with a certain degree of relief that they enrolled me in the high school at Briercrest Bible Institute in Caronport, Saskatchewan.

How I thank God for that decision and their sacrifice. It was there that I finally began to understand what the Christian life was really about and how Jesus is the Way, the Truth and the Life. To live life to its fullest, I had to live it with Jesus, the Giver of life.

That discovery launched me onto an unknown and unfamiliar path expressly designed by a patient and loving Heavenly Father for this sometimes rebellious child.

* * *

I looked at the list before me—all the nursing schools across Canada that accepted students before they reached 18 years of age. As I thought about my future as a missionary, I had decided that I could be most useful as a nurse. I closed my eyes, ran my finger down the page and determined that the school it stopped at would be the one I would attend.

God had mercy on me in this unorthodox decision-making process and through it led me to the Royal Alexandra School of Nursing in Edmonton, Alberta.

One of my new friends there was the daughter of an Alliance pastor in the area and we began to attend Beulah Alliance Church. It was there that I first heard of Alliance missions and finally became convinced that God wanted me to be a missionary with The Christian and Missionary Alliance.

I dreamed of being a missionary nurse in Africa but by this time I had fallen in love with nursing and missionary had become secondary. Instead of using my time to prepare spiritually for my future, I tried to pack into life all the experiences I thought I would have to give up when I became a missionary!

Thankfully many faithful Christians invested their time and love in me and in 1964 I enrolled at Canadian Bible College. I was appalled to see how shallow and distorted my Christian life was. When I was given the responsibility of cleaning the washroom in the ladies residence, I found out that even the basics of Christian living had escaped me!

During my second year at the college I was devastated to discover that the Alliance had very little medical work at that time and the chances of my going out as a missionary nurse with them was not very good. I didn't object to the idea of being a single missionary off in some isolated post, but I did object to the idea of not being a missionary nurse.

I argued long and hard with the Lord. Finally I was able to put my nursing on the altar and tell Him that I would do whatever He wanted me to do.

During my senior year at college I became totally disillusioned with the dating scene. No one I went out with seemed to be headed in the same direction I was. Wasn't it futile to pursue relationships that really didn't have a future? Besides, the vision I had of myself in missionary service did not include housekeeping, having children and assuming the other responsibilities that come with marriage.

Finally, in November, I prayed: "Lord, I'm open to date the one You have chosen to be my life partner, but I don't want to date anyone else anymore." I also prayed that if I was to be married the Lord would prompt someone to invite me to the Christmas banquet. A few days later I received an invitation from Dave.

I knew this was the leading of God. Six dates later we were engaged and in September we were married.

Dave became my spiritual mentor, my best friend and a continual stimulus to growth and development. His encouragement provided the motivation I needed to launch out into new areas of ministry. It was he who pushed me to take those first steps down the unfamiliar paths that have marked our years together. And his servant attitude has taught me much more than any Bible college course.

The Lord knew I needed a partner with a more restless and adventurous spirit than mine. Keeping up with him, as you will see, has been a challenge!

3

Expelled

(David)

"**I** can't believe you've been kicked out of Bible school!" The phrase played over and over during the next few days as my friends tried to console me. I could hardly believe it myself. How could this have happened?

I had grown up in a wonderful Christian home and had accepted the Lord when I was just five. I had attended church all my life.

When my family moved to southern Alberta in 1960 I started attending a Christian and Missionary Alliance Church in the nearby city of Lethbridge. One spring a group of young people from the church attended the annual youth conference at Canadian Bible College in Regina. CBC, I decided, was the place for me.

I had no ambition to pursue a career and, even if I had, my grades were not good enough to get into university. Bible school looked like a good filler until I got serious about my future.

Although things looked good on the outside, my Christian life was not really all that satisfying to me. I spent a lot of time feeling guilty about my lack of discipline and victory. I was drifting along like the prairie tumbleweeds and just couldn't seem to get my life on track. I assumed that God would have little interest in using someone like me in ministry.

My second year at Bible college brought things to a head. A spur-of-the-moment decision to sneak off campus and stay out all night with three other students brought us face to face a few days later with the Student Life Committee. We were all placed on "room campus" for one month. This meant that we could not leave our rooms except for meals, classes, church and bathroom visits.

By the end of the month, two of us had accummulated enough violations to require further discipline. Once again, there had been nothing premeditated. The violations just "happened." My lack of seriousness in my Christian walk had finally projected me to a place of crisis.

When the verdict was handed down in an official letter from the school, I suddenly realized where my drifting had taken me. First, I would have to tell my Christian parents that their son had been kicked out of Bible school. Then I would have to go back to my home church and inform them that I would no longer be needing the scholarship funds they had been providing to help me through school. And last, and maybe worst of all, I would have to figure out what to do with my life.

I decided to look for a job up north in Churchill, Manitoba and, since I had nowhere to stay, Pastor Les Hamm and his wife Shirley invited me to stay with them. Through the encouragement of this godly couple I began to seek God for His will in my life.

One morning, as I sat on a large rock overlooking the chilly waters of Hudson Bay, God spoke clearly to me through His Word, calling me into ministry. It was hard to believe, considering my credentials. What did I have to offer? Absolutely nothing. I hadn't yet learned that God delights in taking the weak and making them strong.

A letter asking for forgiveness and the opportunity for a fresh start was all that was needed to get me back in college for the fall semester. I had lost a semester but it was well worth the lessons I had learned.

I wasn't back at school for more than two months when I became aware that God was asking me to be a missionary. The Friday night missionary meetings that I had earlier found so uninteresting suddenly took on great significance. Hardly a week went by that the Lord didn't confirm in some way that this was the direction He wanted me to take.

I had no doubt that the most fantastic years of my life lay directly ahead of me. At last I had a purpose for living.

4

La Ronge

(Arlene)

"Enter at your own risk!" The sign was crudely printed on a piece of paper and attached to the door frame with the blade of a hunting knife jammed into the wood.

We had just arrived in La Ronge, Saskatchewan to begin two years of home service before receiving our missionary assignment. The president of the church board was on hand to take us on a tour of the parsonage.

It was a huge unfinished house sitting on a rock overlooking the lake. The view from the large living room window was spectacular, with blue water framed by forests and hills in various shades of green.

I was impressed with the size of the house. It was at least three or four times the size of the basement apartment we had left in Regina.

In contrast to the rest of the house, the second bedroom upstairs was full of personal items which indicated that someone was living there. The sight of that knife and the crude sign on the doorframe was a shock not only to us but to the chairman of the board as well.

"I guess he hasn't moved out yet," he observed. "We told him to be out by today."

"He" was a young man who had been led to the Lord by the former pastor. He had lived with the pastor's family until they left La Ronge and was very obviously still making himself at home in the parsonage.

That evening we were in the process of trying to organize the few things we owned when the door opened and in walked Jack.

Although surprised that he had walked in without knocking, we invited him into the near-empty living room. He sat down on the sole piece of furniture—an old trunk—and silently looked us over.

We tried to make conversation. He didn't respond, but just kept looking at us, his eyes intermittently darting around the room. We felt as if we were being weighed in the balance and found wanting.

"Do you like young people?" he finally asked, breaking the silence.

Before we could stammer out an answer, he added: "Pastor Clint liked young people."

Scrutinizing the room further, he began to tell us how the former pastor had arranged the house: "The sofa was over there and the . . . ." His eyes slowly made a circuit of the room as he described everything as it had been in place only days before.

It soon became evident that we, not he, were the intruders in the parsonage. We were intruding in the sanctuary of his memories.

A few days later he moved his things out of the house but that was not the end of Jack. In the weeks that followed we often found signs of his having been there. He had been a burglar before his conversion and boasted that there wasn't a lock in the whole town that was too difficult for him. With that information in mind, we decided it would be a waste of money to change the locks on the house.

A dirty dish in the sink, an empty milk carton on the cupboard, some item moved just a bit from its normal place—these were often the only evidence that sometime during the night, while we were sleeping, Jack had been in. He slept on the floor in the living room, disdaining the offer to use the sofa or the bed in the extra room upstairs.

Many days when Dave went to the church to study he would find things rearranged as the former pastor had them when he studied there—the chair facing the window, the items on the table placed in his special way—continuous reminders that we were intruding on Jack's sacred territory.

In the meantime, we began to learn some things about pastoring. We were astounded at how poorly prepared we were for the reality of the pastorate. I had never attended a ladies' missionary meeting and had no idea what went on there. I had never been a Sunday school superintendent and had not taken much interest in the Christian Education courses at Bible college. After all, what did a missionary nurse need to know about that kind of thing?

Dave, only 22 years old, had done his student

ministry preaching, but that hadn't prepared him for preaching two sermons a week, plus giving the Bible study at the midweek prayer meeting. And we had had no experience with working with youth—we had only been youth!

The one thing we did know was that God had called us to pastor the church in La Ronge. We desperately hoped that He would somehow provide what we needed.

One night a few months after we moved into the parsonage our frequent silent visitor appeared and told Dave that he was finally willing to accept him as his pastor and would no longer attempt to sabotage our efforts. That was good news. Things were beginning to improve.

The people that lived in the small houses sprawled around the hill on which the parsonage was perched began to respond to their new neighbors. Dave was able to lead several to the Lord.

One day a young woman came running up to the house. Her grandmother was dying and she needed help. The people in the neighborhood knew that I worked at the small local hospital.

Dave and I went down to the shack and found an ancient, emaciated, deathly pale woman sitting in a chair with blood-soaked rags and towels surrounding her. Her nose was bleeding profusely.

We discovered that she had extremely high blood pressure and had stopped taking her medicine. I tried to stem the flow of blood with all the emergency techniques I knew. It was useless.

We urged her to let us take her to the hospital for treatment. She didn't speak English and her

granddaughter didn't need to interpret her reply
after she heard our suggestion. She vehemently
shook her head and riveted her dark eyes on us. If
she was going to die, we were told, she wanted to
die at home.

Not knowing what else to do, Dave laid his hands
on her and began to pray, asking God to do the impossible. Immediately the bleeding stopped. We
were stunned, astounded at the quiet, ever-present
power of God.

Each time we met her after that she took our
hands in hers and greeted us with an effusive
"thank you" in her native Cree language. God was
teaching us that our only adequecy would be found
in dependence on Him and His power.

The winter in La Ronge was bitterly cold and the
unfinished parsonage was almost impossible to
heat. At what seemed then to be great personal
sacrifice we saved enough money to buy a cheap
rug to put on the bare living room floor to bring a
bit of warmth to the room. I kept it impeccably
clean so that our firstborn, Kurt, could crawl and
play on it instead of on the cold floor.

We had the only telephone in that area of town
and so our phone became the public phone for the
whole neighborhood. People came at all hours to
use it.

The phone had been installed in the living room
but when we bought the rug for that room I had
the phone company move it into the kitchen. That
way, I thought, the public traffic would be in the
kitchen that was easier to clean and my precious
rug would be spared.

The first person to come to use the phone was a lady who had just come in from the trapline. Her boots were laden with mud and dirt from the bush. As she walked into the kitchen, leaving great clumps of slimy mud on the floor, I silently congratulated myself on the wisdom of putting the phone in the kitchen.

She had just finished her call when Kurt, who had been playing in the living room, made some kind of noise.

"Oh, let me see your baby," the woman exclaimed, clumping across the rug toward Kurt. I never was able to remove the stains of that mud from the rug!

Slowly but surely I was learning that those Christ died for were so much more important than any material thing I might possess and that whatever I owned was given to me to be shared as an extension of my ministry.

It was a lesson I would recall many times in the years that followed.

5

On Our Way

(Arlene)

Dave was exuberant as we drove down the highway leading south out of La Ronge. We were on our way to the mission field at last!

About a month earlier we had received that wonderful letter from Mission headquarters: "You have been appointed to Colombia. Be prepared to start language study in Costa Rica in August of this year."

For 18 months we had anxiously awaited our appointment—the culmination of our years of study and home service. Suddenly we could envision the fulfillment of our goal of being missionaries. But we scarcely knew what that meant.

The final application forms had had a space labelled "preferred field." We had no answer. Dave studied and prayed over a map of the world along with the Alliance prayer manual and felt that Brazil would be a good option. The Alliance was just getting started there and the idea of being a pioneer appealed to him.

So we marked Brazil as our first choice but left the final decision up to those at the Mission office. We felt that they were in a better position to make it than we were.

When the letter came appointing us to Colombia we thanked the Lord for His leading and then ran for a map. All we knew about Colombia was that it was somewhere in South America.

As we rolled down the unpaved highway out of La Ronge the cloud of dust we left behind fell like a curtain on that period of our lives and ministry.

Memories. We had been in La Ronge for almost two years and we left feeling less than successful in ministry. Certainly it had been a learning time but we had never had to battle with pride regarding our time there. The brethren had sent us off with their blessing and probably a good deal of relief.

Our memories were not of those that we had ministered to but of those who had ministered to us. We remembered the special couple who decided that their ministry would be befriending the pastor and his wife. Many times they would return to the church after everyone else had left and we were locking up, with an invitation to go to their house for lunch or coffee. Their home was a place where we could relax and laugh and know that we were accepted and loved even with all our flaws.

We would also miss the fresh bread that the missionary to the Indians so often had waiting when I went to pick up Kurt after a day of work at the hospital. She not only provided us with wonderful homemade bread but a secure place to leave Kurt while I worked.

We would miss the moose meat and other game given to us from the hunters in the congregation. But I wouldn't miss the huge moose liver that filled the whole sink. I never did learn to cook that in a way that made it palatable!

We would miss the young people who had become part of our lives and taught us so many things we needed to know with their innocent frankness.

While these memories served to warm our hearts, we couldn't help but experience a great sense of relief. We felt as if a heavy burden had rolled off us. Our trial of home service was over. We had not done it as well as we could have but it had been accepted—another evidence that the purposes of God are not thwarted by the frailty of man.

We were on our way!

6

Passing the Faith Test

(Arlene)

Excitement was high at the language school. The topic of conversation in the classrooms, at the coffee breaks and on the buses was singular: What are your plans for Christmas vacation? Over 100 language students preparing for ministry in Latin America were gearing up for a much-needed break.

The Christmas season marked the end of the honeymoon period of living in an exotic, foreign country. The prospect of a lifetime of missionary service far away from family and friends had already begun to take its emotional toll. Some of the more fortunate students had received the Christmas present of a trip back home, postponing for a while the reality of the future.

Others, deciding to make the best of it, were planning to spend their vacation traveling throughout Costa Rica, experiencing the beauty and the culture of that picturesque country, perhaps even practicing the little Spanish they'd learned in the past few months.

Dave and I were quiet when we found ourselves in the middle of these conversations. We knew that we would neither be going home for Christmas nor traveling to some exotic tourist spot. The truth was we were broke. We didn't have the money to do anything. We had not yet learned to live within the limits of our missionary allowance and while we had budgeted our money to meet our needs and pay our bills for the month of December we were caught off guard and without reserves when we were informed that Costa Rican law demanded an extra half month's salary for our maid in December.

Rita, the helpful Christian lady who came in every day to look after two-year-old Kurt while we went to classes, definitely needed the money for her family. There was no question in our minds that the right thing to do was to take our grocery money for the last two weeks of December and give it to her, thus fulfilling our legal obligations. We had already relinquished any thoughts of traveling or buying Christmas presents, but now things were getting serious!

We had not responded well to an earlier financial crunch just two months after arriving in Costa Rica. Our missionary allowance from New York had not arrived in the mail on the date we expected it. We had been left with no money.

We prayed and went expectantly to the post office every day, confident that the check would be there. Finally Friday came. We realized that if the check wasn't there we would have to wait until Monday when the post office reopened after the weekend.

On Friday the mailbox once again failed to produce the check. By this time we had used up the odds and ends of groceries that we had in the house and were down to a bit of milk and about a half pound of flour.

We did our best to be positive about it. Dave and I could easily make it through a weekend without eating. There was milk for Kurt and I could use that bit of flour to make bread and thus we could survive until our allowance arrived.

We faced the weekend stoically. I had already suggested to Dave on several occasions during the week that we confide our need to our friends and get help from them, but he felt that we should just pray and trust the Lord to provide. He had learned many lessons of faith in his home as a child but for me this was a new experience. I was not particularly enjoying living by faith.

On Saturday morning I went into the kitchen to prepare Kurt's breakfast. The scene that confronted me dissipated the last shred of my faltering hope.

I had stored the flour in a cookie tin canister on the counter. Kurt, seeing the pretty pictures of the cookies on the can, had used a chair to climb up and get a cookie. I found him with the can open, the flour dumped out on the floor.

What would I do now? I would have swept it up, sifted it and used it anyway, but Kurt was sitting in the middle of it in a wet diaper! I had no alternative but to throw out the flour and with it my last resolve to trust God to provide.

That morning we borrowed money from friends and bought enough food to tide us over until Monday. It was a long and miserable weekend. We knew we had failed our faith test.

The pain of that failure was intense. Our faith—*my* faith particularly—had not really been in God but in that bit of flour. When the flour was gone, so was our faith. Dave and I talked and prayed about it, confessed our lack of faith and determined that when the next test came we would pass.

Now, two months later, with a long, lonely, cashless Christmas ahead of us, we were once again wondering where our daily bread would come from.

Every morning found us at the post office to see if God had provided for our need through a family member or friend. All around us were exclamations of pleasure and "Praise the Lord!" from our fellow students as they opened their mail and found those precious gifts tucked away inside letters and Christmas cards.

But not for the Peters. As has happened so often in our ministry, God decided to surprise us by doing something completely unexpected.

A few days before classes were to end for the holiday season, Dave noticed a sign posted on the bulletin board: "Jamaican, English-speaking church in Porto Limon (a coastal city) needs preacher over the Christmas season." The sign also mentioned that the church was prepared to pay the airfare for the preacher and his family, provide a place to stay and food for a two-week period!

I don't remember how much we prayed about it, but one week later we were on our way to the coast. The sky was clear as we flew over the mountains and caught our first glimpse of the emerald-green Caribbean. We landed parallel to the beach with only a row of tall palm trees separating us from the ocean. We felt as if we had landed in paradise.

An elder from the church met us and drove us to the place where we would be staying for the next two weeks. We had expected to stay with a family from the church. How delighted we were when we pulled up to a huge house two blocks off the beach and were informed that this was the manse, our home for the next two weeks. And, since the church was without a pastor, we would have the house to ourselves and a lady from the church would come in each day to prepare our meals!

Dave's duties consisted of preaching on Christmas Day and on New Year's Eve. The rest of the time was ours—a dream vacation provided by God.

Days were spent walking on deserted or sparsely populated beaches, swimming in the ocean, eating the fabulous creole food our cook prepared, savoring turtle meat for the first time, trying out our Spanish on the local populace and sitting on one of the balconies of the manse observing the life and movement of the city.

Evenings were spent basking in the warm breezes off the beach, listening to the strong but comforting sounds of the waves relentlessly pounding the shore, watching the bobbing lights of the ships in port, imagining from what exotic ports they had come. Our spirits, minds and bodies rested and luxuriated in God's provision.

Christmas day dawned, our first one away from the homeland. Would we be overcome with homesickness here so far away from all that was familiar and loved, we wondered.

The order of the day was first to give Kurt the plastic toy I had bought for him for a bit less than a dollar. His delight with the gift was priceless and the little plastic train travelled many miles in his hand.

Our breakfast of Christmas pudding and breads had been left the day before. Our hearts burst in sincere thankfulness to God for the gift of His Son.

The Christmas service was so incredibly special as the congregation came to greet us and wish us their Jamaican version of Merry Christmas— "Felicitations of the Season." In spite of the tropical heat, the people arrived in suits and ties and extravagant dresses fit for the biggest social event of the year. The service was conducted with all the pomp and ceremony that their British heritage demanded.

A pump organ accompanied the choirs and the organist was soon drenched in perspiration. Dave, preaching for the first time in four months, was amazed at how much sweat the human body can produce when encased in a suit and tie in humid tropical heat!

It was a small price to pay for the privilege of sharing Christmas with these wonderful folk in their cultural celebration of the birth of Christ. After the service we were invited to Christmas dinner in the home of the church elder and had wonderful fellowship with him and his family. A slight twinge of guilt crowded in on the pleasure of the day as we returned to our house that night—we had not once missed our homeland!

Back in San Jose, we were no longer silent in the conversation groups at language school. We couldn't keep quiet about God's surprising provision for our first Christmas away from home and family. Money could not have bought it!

And besides, we had finally passed a faith test that would serve us well in the days ahead.

7

The "Sober" Bus

(David)

"When will you be back?" Arlene asked as she gave me one last kiss before I climbed into the Jeep.

"One week from today," I promised her assuringly. I should have added, "If God so wills!"

Our first assignment in Colombia was to the city of Ibague. One of my responsibilities was to visit the Alliance churches scattered throughout the provinces (called departments) of Tolima and Huila. While many of these could be reached by car, a number of them required a combination of two or three different modes of transportation. Bilbao was one of those places.

The Bilbao Alliance Church was about to dedicate their new church building and I had been invited to participate. Two Colombian pastors accompanied me as we headed south by Jeep towards the small city of Chaparral. From there we would board a one-engine plane to Herrera, a town nestled high in the Andes mountains and from there we would have a four-hour horseback ride to Bilbao.

The half-day Jeep trip to Chaparral passed without incident and we were soon surveying the Beaver aircraft that was to take us to Herrera.

This wasn't the first time I had flown in a small plane since arriving in Colombia a few months earlier, so I knew what to expect. We would be flying "through" the Andes and not over them. I would experience sheer terror as the air currents knocked us around. I would lose my lunch within the hour and we would probably be landing on a ridiculously short airstrip carved out of the side of a mountain.

Today, however, the trip was mercifully short and my lunch was still in place when I spotted what seemed to be the airstrip below us. Both ends and one side were precipitous cliffs. The other side was mountain. And it was obviously too short to land on!

Our pilot, undeniably braver than I was, started his descent. In his first attempt at landing, the wheels never quite got down to ground level. On his second attempt he came down so hard that we bounced right back up, so around we went again.

By this time I was confessing all past, present and future sins to the Lord. The two pastors with me appeared to be doing the same.

The third attempt at landing was a resounding success. How good it felt to come to a stop, to step out of the plane and to set our feet on solid ground.

It was too late in the afternoon to continue on to Bilbao so we decided to have a service in Herrera that night. I was amazed to see the church fill up by meeting time even though there had been only a couple of hours to let people in the area know about the service. A number of Christians who had not attended church in months, or in some cases years, were there that night and made new commitments to the Lord.

Many times during our years in Colombia I would marvel that just the visit of a missionary in a town or village served as a catalyst to bring backslidden people back to God. Often it had been a missionary that had brought the gospel to them in the first place and they would be reminded of their original commitment to God.

The next morning some small but sure-footed horses carried us safely along the narrow mountain paths to our final destination, Bilbao. For the rest of the week we had Bible classes during the day and services at night.

The church was led by a layman and it had been three years since the last visit from a pastor or missionary. Yet in that time the believers had remained faithful to the Lord. The new facilities had been built at considerable sacrifice and now there was great rejoicing as the celebrations continued on into the weekend.

The Herrera Church had asked if I could be back there to preach in their Sunday morning service, so on Saturday I made my way back over the mountain trails, this time on foot.

Passing the Herrera airstrip on my way into town I noticed that the plane that had brought us in was sitting off to the side of the runway. What caught my eye was the fact that it was missing a wing! I soon found out what had happened.

On Wednesday of that week the plane had over-shot the runway and when the pilot realized that he would run out before being able to stop, he turned the plane into the side of the mountain, ripping off one wing and damaging the propeller.

No one was hurt and by the next day the airline had put another plane into service. It looked like our trip out on Monday would not be jeopardized.

I woke up Sunday morning thinking of home. Tomorrow I would be holding Arlene in my arms. I would be telling Kurt about the horses I had ridden, about the airplane ride that had terrorized me. I wondered if baby Karla would remember me.

We had just finished our morning service and I was having lunch with a family from the church when the news reached us: "An airplane has crashed on the runway!"

We ran out of the house and joined a stream of townspeople hurrying towards the airstrip.

This time things were a little more serious. The pilot had touched down too late and, realizing he would run out of runway, had tried to lift off again. Not having sufficient speed for a proper takeoff, the plane lost altitude and crashed into the side of a mountain 200 yards away.

The pilot and three of the passengers died instantly. Four other passengers were seriously injured. It was a tremendous blow for the small town.

I spent the afternoon practicing what little first aid I knew and praying with family members and friends of those involved in the accident. Later that day a rescue helicopter arrived and evacuated the injured to Bogota.

The next day the town received word that the airstrip had been closed down until the accident could be investigated. This meant that we would have to walk out to the town of Rio Blanco and catch a bus from there to Chaparral where we had left the Jeep.

It would be a two-day walk to Rio Blanco and I was not looking foward to it. I was also agonizing over the fact that Arlene would hear about the crash and wonder if I had been on that plane, especially since I wouldn't be showing up when she expected me. And then there was the matter of my stomach. I was not feeling well and could not eat anything at all.

I was surprised at how much strength the Lord gave me during the next day and a half as I walked up and down mountain trails, unable to eat and suffering the effects of dysentery. A full moon allowed us to continue our trip through a good part of Monday night. We reached Rio Blanco at one o'clock Tuesday afternon and went to the home of a Christian lady.

"I have been fasting and praying that the Lord would send someone who could have a service with us," she said exuberantly. "So tonight we will get the Christians together here in my house."

We explained that we were already two days late getting home and we would have to leave on the bus that afternoon. She was disappointed and wondered aloud why the Lord would lead her to fast and pray if He wasn't going to answer her prayer.

We found out that there were two buses in town

and that they would be leaving any minute. Both bus drivers had been drinking. We chose the one who appeared the least drunk. The fact that he would be driving along narrow mountain roads did not seem to bother him or the other passengers so we decided to take the risk.

We had been on the road for over an hour when the bus suddenly veered off to one side and came to a stop. When the driver stood up with the steering wheel in his hand I realized that we would not be going much farther in this bus!

Five minutes later the second bus pulled alongside us and we climbed in. This driver was almost completely drunk and the passengers started urging me to take over the wheel. I was the only other person there that knew how to drive so it seemed like the logical thing to do. The driver, who was also the owner of the other vehicle, finally agreed to this arrangement.

The bus (actually it was a truck with some benches in it) was heavily loaded both with people and huge sacks of rice. I slid confidently into the driver's seat.

As we crept into motion I tried to shift from first gear into second and soon realized that this was not quite like driving a car. The bus came to a complete stop as I struggled with the gear shift.

Then before I hardly knew what was happening, we were rolling backward!

I hit the brakes but the pedal went right to the floor. The driver yelled something which I understood as "the brakes don't work." Later I found out that he was telling me I needed to pump the brakes, but by this time I was concentrating on what was behind me and the rolling bus.

One side of the road went straight down and the other side straight up. I chose the "up" side in the hopes that it would help me bring the bus to a stop. A couple of fellows standing on the back bumper jumped off just before we crashed into the side of the mountain.

Everyone got out to survey the damage and the bus driver let loose a string of Spanish words I had not learned in language school. The bus would need some work done on it before it could be used again.

The driver was not happy. Neither were the rest of us although we were thankful to the Lord for sparing our lives. There would be no more buses out of Rio Blanco that day and we would obviously not be making it home that night.

Eventually a bus came by heading to Rio Blanco. So back we went.

"I knew the Lord would answer my prayers!" the señora exclaimed ecstatically. She quickly rounded up a group of people and that night, as God blessed the preaching of His Word, we soon forgot our anxiety about getting home.

The next day we caught a "sober" bus to Chaparral, climbed gratefully into the Jeep and four hours later were back with our families.

It was good to be home!

8

Contemplating Widowhood

(Arlene)

W*hy isn't Dave home yet?* I wondered as the three of us waited impatiently. He had been gone a week and we missed him. Kurt was three years old and Karla only a few months old.

Well, I would bake a batch of cookies as a "welcome home" present. Dave usually came home from those trips craving sweets. This time I would be ready.

It was almost supper time when my neighbor knocked on the door.

"Has Dave come home yet?" she asked.

When she heard that he had not, she added, "I don't want to alarm you but I read in the newspaper today about a plane accident in Herrera last night."

Responding to my ignorance and surprise, she ran home and got the paper. Sure enough. There had been an accident at the airport in Herrera.

Several passengers as well as the pilot had been killed and several others had been seriously injured. The time of the accident coincided with the time I assumed Dave would be leaving to come home.

I took consolation in the fact that the paper, while it didn't list the names of the victims, also did not state "Gringo killed in plane crash." Surely if a foreigner had been killed out there in the Andean wilderness it would have been mentioned.

My neighbor offered to drive over to the nearest police post to see if they had any further word on the accident. Nothing. I could only adopt the attitude of wait and see.

Israel, the local pastor, was on the trip with Dave. His wife Marta came over to see what I knew. Marta was a fairly young Christian and I tried to calm her with assuring phrases and Scripture verses that I was having a hard time believing myself.

Eventually she seemed to relax enough for us to pray together and she returned home. We agreed to contact each other whenever we had news. In the meantime we needed to pray and trust the Lord to bring our men home.

Night crept slowly on. I tried to turn my growing fear over to the Lord but with the passing of hours the possibility of Dave not returning became more real. When I finally did go to sleep for a short time I dreamed he was lying injured in a crevasse in the mountains where the searchers couldn't find him.

In the morning my neighbor was at the house bright and early with the morning newspaper. The only thing the paper reported was that the airport at Herrera had been closed until several recent accidents there could be investigated.

I spent the day pretending. I pretended that nothing was unusual when Kurt asked, "When is Daddy coming home?"

"Maybe today," I responded as optimistically as possible. "Let's pray that he does." Then I would leave him with his books and toys and go into the bathroom to cry, overwhelmed with fear. I was glad Kurt was young enough to accept the cheery words I had for him when I finally emerged again.

I pretended when Marta came over about noon. Panic was written on her face and it was obvious that she had been crying.

"Our husbands are in God's hands," I comforted her. "He will look after them." I hoped she wouldn't see my lack of confidence in what I was telling her. We prayed together again.

When she left I went back to the bathroom where I could close and lock the door so Kurt wouldn't see me crying.

This time when I came out I felt as if there really was little hope of things working out "right" in this situation. Dave was now two days late. No news was not good news to me.

Anytime now there will be a policeman at my door telling me that my husband has been killed. What will I do then? I found myself asking. Other similar thoughts kept racing through my mind.

Realizing that when the now seemingly inevitable news came I might not be capable of making rational decisions, I sat down with a piece of paper to list the things I had to do: Contact Mission headquarters in Cali. (I'd have to send a telegram. We had no phone.) Have them notify our families. Arrange to sell everything. (I felt I couldn't stay on the field with two small children and be of any use at that time.) And so the list went on, including how to dispose of our Pekinese puppy.

By this time my trips to the bathroom were characterized by anger more than grief. *Lord, how can You do this to me? You bring me down to this country and leave me alone with two little kids? It isn't fair!*

Night once again fell without news. By this time I was sure I was a widow. I went to bed but I didn't sleep. I cried. I raged. I accused God of injustice. I grieved. I didn't want to spend the rest of my life without Dave. I tried to pray but my emotions kept taking control.

In the early hours of the morning I was in a rage stage. *How can You do this to me? I need Dave. The kids need a father. It's not right!*

Then, suddenly, in the middle of the struggle I heard God speak to me.

"He's mine, you know," He said quietly. "I can do with him as I please."

The room was filled with the strong comforting presence of God. The rage and questioning gave way as an incredible peace flowed over me and I heard myself responding, "I know. Whatever You choose is all right with me."

That submission brought a serenity and trust I hadn't experienced for days. Maybe I was a widow. Maybe my children had lost their father. But we were not alone.

In the morning when Marta came over I was able to comfort and encourage her in a very different way and the Lord ministered to her.

The incredible happiness of seeing Dave at the door later that day defied description. He was unshaven, dirty, haggard and gaunt from his trek and illness. But he was alive.

Later, as he told me his side of the story, we could see how God had ordered his steps and had literally done with him as He chose.

I told him of my meeting with God, an experience that became a foundation of peace and assurance whenever he travelled throughout the years of our missionary experience.

And whenever I was tempted to yield to fear I remembered the words of the Lord: "He's mine, you know."

9

Caesarean with
a Machete

(Arlene)

"I just did a Caesarean section! Unfortunately, mother and babies did not survive."

I could hardly believe what I was hearing myself say.

There are things we are called upon to do as missionaries for which no training or experience has prepared us. This was one of those occasions.

We had been abruptly transferred from the city of Ibague to the Indian Bible Institute at Silvia due to the sudden illness of the resident missionary. Dave and I were anything but prepared for the responsibilities that faced us there.

We had been in Colombia a bit more than a year and had just finished our second year of language study requirements. Dave had previously indicated to the executive committee that sometime in the future we would like to help out in the Indian work. A month later we received a phone call from the field chairman asking if we could be ready to move in two weeks!

It was a scramble but we made it. Within our first hours at Silvia we began to feel we had bitten off more than we could chew.

The Bible institute, known as Ambachico, was located on a small farm just outside the town of Silvia in southwest Colombia. Dave, as the director, would be responsible for the operation of the farm, running the Bible institute and overseeing the more than 50 congregations in the Paez and Guambiano tribes.

I would teach in the Bible institute, be the school nurse and look after the many guests and visitors the Bible school attracted.

While I unpacked barrels and set up the house, Dave was out learning how things were done on the farm.

The first thing he faced was a huge ancient generator that was the source of electricity for the farm. It was run by water power and had to be regulated manually several times a day to keep our appliances and light bulbs from burning out.

We learned to recognize by the smell of the sizzling insects on the lightbulbs when it was running too high. Dave would then sprint over to the plant to make the necessary adjustment.

When the rains came, the water canals that fed the power plant either turned into raging torrents that raised the voltage too high or were blocked up by landslides and debris, shutting down the generator altogether. Over the years we began to suspect that the machine used up more energy to keep it running than it produced for our use.

Second item on the tour was a trip around the

farm learning about the dangers of pasturing the cows on the steep hillsides. Several animals, Dave was told, had fallen off the switchbacking trails and broken their necks.

In addition, the plateau on the top of the mountain behind the institute buildings was in constant danger of invasion by members of a radical political group operating in the area.

In a large fenced-in section on the main area of the farm there were several pigs. They were part of a special project of the Wycliffe missionaries in cooperation with the two tribes in the area.

The huge purebred boar had been flown in from the States along with several females of the same breed for the purpose of developing a better strain for marketing. But they required all kinds of special attention and care. Both Dave and I were duly impressed with their fragility.

We had never lived on a farm and the responsibility of caring for such a crucial and expensive project was a bit overwhelming. Fortunately the farm foreman knew more about these things than we did.

As the weeks passed we began to feel as if we had at least a general idea of what was going on. I stayed far from the pigs and the cows and dedicated myself to teaching and to the guest house ministries. That is, until one day when the foreman came running up to the house looking for Don (Mr.) David. Since he wasn't there, I asked him what the problem was.

"One of the sows is in labor and is unable to give birth," he responded breathlessly.

Suddenly the nursing instinct in me took over and I ran out to the pig area with him. It was obvious at first glance that the sow was near death. I was so concerned about what would happen with the project that I decided that we had to at least try to save the piglets.

I had the foreman and the hired man put the moribund sow on her back and hold her as I performed a Caeserean section with the foreman's machete. Having worked for several years in an operating room I had a general idea of the procedure for humans. Surely it couldn't be too much different for a sow!

Unfortunately, each piglet I delivered was dead and the operation turned into an autopsy as I discovered a dead fetus lodged in the birth canal. It had been dead for some time and had obviously poisoned its mother and its siblings.

It would have been interesting to listen in on the conversations around the fires that night by those who had participated in or observed my surgery.

In our house, once we realized that it didn't mean the end of the pig project, we joked about this not being part of our job description.

✦ ✦ ✦

Some months later the Lord used that same pig project to teach us another valuable lesson. Watching the other sows give birth and the piglets being sold in the marketplace for a good price, we began to think that a little entrepreneurship might work. Why couldn't we, too, buy a female piglet, raise it, breed it and make a bit extra to supplement our missionary allowance? We even had just the right spot beside the house to put it.

We decided to proceed with the plan.

The sow grew beautifully and every time we looked out the window at her or fed her we envisioned growing profits. The day came when we bred her with the huge boar and three months later six beautiful black and white piglets were born.

We checked the going price at the market and excitedly calculated our prospective profits.

Then one by one the piglets got sick and died.

"Well," we reasoned, "we can always breed her again and maybe next time we'll have better luck."

Not so.

The sow herself also got sick and died. Thus ended our first and last effort to run a private business on the side. How easy it would have been for us to get sidetracked from the work God had called us to do.

10

Love Your Neighbor

(Arlene)

Getting up the long winding driveway to the Indian Bible Institute was often a trip in itself.

The turn off the main road was marked with a shrine to the Virgin Mary. Years before, when the Alliance had purchased the Ambachico farm for the purpose of establishing a center for the work with the Paez and Guambiano tribes, the shrine had been built at the edge of the property by the townspeople to prevent the spread of the heretical evangelical religion into the town.

The statue of the virgin embracing the Christchild was kept in good repair and almost always had bouquets of fresh flowers in the vases at its base. The town's fanatical resistance to the gospel over the years sometimes gave us the impression that the shrine was accomplishing its purpose.

A few yards further up the road was a not-so-well kept monument to Simon Bolivar, the great liberator of Colombia from Spanish domination years before. The legend on the monument marked our property as one of the places he and his army had passed through and spent the night on one of his famous liberation treks.

Not too far from the monument was a small shack made of cardboard and bits of wood and tin rescued from the town garbage. It was the home of the town "loco," Congola.

Mentally deranged and rejected by family, Congola had built his shack on the edge of our property and from there made his daily begging excursions into the town. We often sent food down from the Bible institute to help him.

Rumors in town and stories spread by those opposed to the gospel were that anyone embracing the religion of the evangelicals would go crazy. Congola's residence at the entrance to our driveway appeared to confirm the rumors.

The driveway was lined with towering eucalyptus trees and with the "living" fences typical of that area of Colombia. Posts cut from a tree called the *lechera* were stuck in the ground and barbed wire strung between them. Shortly after the fence was "planted" those posts would take root and grow into trees. We never had any problem with rotting fenceposts.

On the right side of the steep, winding road was a creek that emptied into a river below. Further to the right of the creek a family had claimed squatter's rights to a triangular piece of land and had built themselves a small house. They pastured their cow on the land and made cheese to sell in the town market.

Whenever we went by we would call out a greeting to them but they would just look away and not answer. Their son was the same age as Kurt and some other boys at the Bible institute, but they refused to allow him to join in their games.

We even allowed the family to hook up to the Bible institute water and electric supply, but that still did not produce any positive communication with them.

One day when the lady was working in her garden I noticed that she was pregnant. I was happy when a few days later the opportunity presented itself to offer my services to her as a nurse. It was received with stony silence.

As the weeks passed it became apparent that she was approaching her due date.

A knock on the door came one night about nine o'clock. Dave opened the door to find the neighbor on the doorstep. He told us his wife was in labor and needed help.

I quickly put some scissors and cord on the stove to boil, grabbed some clean sheets and cloths and ran over to their house.

It had been raining for days and the little creek was full. The single plank bridge over it was off balance and slick. Thankful for the flashlight I had with me I carefully worked my way across it.

I found the neighbor lady in the last stages of labor. A quick examination told me that I would not be the one to deliver that baby. Her bed was a pool of blood and with every contraction more blood gushed out. I was sure she would die without immediate medical help.

Her husband had earlier contacted the village midwife who had come that day, but frightened by the complications had run off and not returned. That was when the neighbor came to ask for help.

We quickly fashioned a stretcher out of a couple of blankets and lifted her onto it. Dave and her husband each took an end and I tried to support the middle. The woman was in a state of terror. I tried to calm her as best I could as she continued to lose blood at an alarming rate.

As we crossed the creek on the way to the Jeep that Dave had pulled up to the edge of the road we slipped, almost dumping the poor woman in the frigid water. This scared her so badly that she quit pushing and began panting, an exercise I had been trying to get her to do from the instant I first examined her.

We finally got her into the back of the car, all the while chasing away their dog as well as several Bible institute dogs that had come around to see what all the excitement was about.

We roared down the driveway to the town clinic less than a mile away. The dogs followed us, barking and howling. I was struck with the hilarity of the situation. We had no siren on our "ambulance" but the dogs performed that function, alerting all to stay out of our way.

We pulled up to the small building that served as the hospital and I ran in to get help. A nursing aide was sitting at a table in the entry. She looked up casually.

"We have a woman in labor in the car. We need the doctor right away!" I exclaimed, hoping to spur her into action.

Responding in slow motion, the aide pointed down a short hall.

"The stretcher is down there," she said without offering any assistance.

I ran down the hall opening every door and looking into every room, frantically trying to find the stretcher. I finally saw it under a pile of rumpled linens in the last room.

I ran back to the entryway with the stretcher, kicking the yelping dogs out of my way as I went.

With the stretcher at the back of the Jeep the men began to lift the now almost-unconscious patient to put her on it. Just as they were about to let her down the stretcher collapsed. I was left holding the top of it as both sets of legs fell to the ground. The men put the patient back in the car and we hammered the stretcher back together. With the woman finally safely on it, we raced back into the clinic.

This time, seeing that the situation really was urgent, the aide accompanied us to the examining room at the end of the hall and within a few seconds the doctor was there taking charge of the situation.

Every Colombian doctor is required after graduation from medical school to give a year's service to an outpost clinic before he is allowed to set up practice in the city. This is sometimes done reluctantly with little real interest in serving the community.

Over the years we had come to expect little from the doctors that came to the town of Silvia. Often from upper or middle class families they found it difficult to adapt to the lack of adequate facilities, help or medicines, to say nothing of the village culture and lifestyle.

We praised God that the doctor was at the clinic that night and not off drinking in the bar as it seemed was his usual practice.

He delivered a healthy baby and by morning the mother's life was out of danger as well.

We waited around to hear the outcome and later, when family members and friends began to arrive to see the new addition, the father proudly introduced us to them and told them how happy he was that we were his neighbors! The woman's parents personally thanked us for helping out in the crisis.

This experience blasted away the wall of resistance they had erected and we became good friends. Every Tuesday after that we received a present of cheese wrapped in banana leaves. Even today, whenever I eat white cheese, I am reminded of that family and how God chose to break down barriers so that His Word could be shared with them.

Though they began to attend the services we held at the Bible institute, as far as we know they never accepted the Lord.

11

Apolinar

(David)

The men sat on small wooden trunks arranged around the fire like chairs around a dining room table. The orange light from the flames flickered on the soot-blackened adobe walls as the smoke filtered up through the bamboo slats that formed the roof of the kitchen.

I had asked Apolinar Yonda, my host and the pastor of the Betania Church, to relate his testimony to me. The other men with me had heard it before but always enjoyed a good story.

The Paez Indian church in Betania was one of the largest and oldest in the tribe. It hosted several regional conferences each year and was without dispute the evangelical center for that area.

The church was set high on the top of a mountain and was surrounded by small farms owned by believers. On a clear night you could see the lights of the city of Cali twinkling in the distance giving the impression that Betania was closer to civilization than it actually was. The nearest road was a three-hour walk away.

I usually enjoyed my trips to Betania. The church was active in evangelism and teaching and the leaders were men of God. Each day ended with sweet coffee and animated conversation around the kitchen fire. I learned much about Paez culture and history as I listened to their tales.

Apolinar was a lay pastor who supported his family by farming a small area close to the church. He was a continual encouragement to the brethren in the whole Paez area and often traveled for days visiting from church to church.

The love of God was evident in his instant smile and he reflected the presence of the indwelling Christ in a way I have seldom seen.

"As a young man," he began, "I became the pastor of the church here in Betania. This was during the time of *la violencia* (the violence), a time of war in Colombia when political and religious leaders used civil unrest as a pretext to burn down churches and in some cases to murder the believers.

"Evangelicals in the more remote areas of Colombia suffered greatly. They were forced to flee their homes and villages and hide themselves in caves and other mountain areas to save their lives.

"Fear led many of my people to abandon their walk with the Lord and the church was almost empty during the services I conducted on Sundays. The people from the congregation were afraid to identify themselves as evangelicals.

"During this time I became ill. Medical help in this area was non-existent and I got worse. Then one morning when my wife tried to waken me she noticed that I was cold. I had quit breathing. I was dead!"

Apolinar threw another log on the fire as he allowed his words to have their effect.

"My wife sent word to the believers in the area that I had died and would be buried that day. Family members and friends began to build my coffin close to where I lay. I could hear their conversations and the hammering of the nails. I was afraid I would be buried alive.

"All the while, I was able to observe my body. I noticed I was as thin as a pencil. I immediately knew that this gaunt, wasted figure I was viewing represented my spiritual life. A long-standing debt that I had been unwilling to pay had sapped my communion with God and left me spiritually wasted.

"I immediately cried out to God that if He would permit me to return to life I would straighten things out with the person I had wronged.

"Suddenly I found myself transported to a place whose beauty far surpassed anything I had ever seen. The intensity and brightness of the color of everything I saw made this world appear dull in comparison.

"When I spoke, instead of normal speech coming from my mouth, it was as if my teeth were making music as I spoke. Later, the common noises of this world seemed so harsh and ugly.

"The aroma of the area was an incredibly sweet fragrance and it too was beyond anything I had experienced before.

"Somehow I knew that even though it was all so

wonderful I wasn't in heaven. I was still in some way tied to my body. The Lord appeared to me and I asked Him to either take me home or let me return to my body. I was afraid of being buried alive.

"The Lord told me to take a message back to the people: If they were not going to be serious about their Christianity then they didn't need a pastor and the Lord would take me home. If they were going to follow the Lord, then I would be allowed to stay with them as their pastor.

"Eight hours had passed since my wife had found me 'dead.' About 80 of the church people had already filled our house and preparations were underway for my burial. It was at this point that I 'came back to life.'

"The first thing I did was to ask forgiveness of the man I had offended. The debt, I promised, would be paid immediately. Then I relayed the message the Lord had given me. There was immediate repentance as people got on their knees and called out to God to forgive them for their backsliding. By the next Sunday I was back in the church preaching."

The Betania Church quickly became the largest and strongest in the area as people all around heard the message God had sent through Apolinar.

He continued to pastor the church and became one of the most faithful workers in the Paez church. He took courses on how to teach his people to read in their native language and seemed always to be on the front line of whatever God was doing in the tribe.

Years later, when the Paez tribe decided to send its first missionary couple to the Kwaiker tribe in southern Colombia, Apolinar and his wife were chosen to go.

12

Nightmare

(David)

I was one of three special speakers at a youth camp in the province of Caqueta. It was more than two days travel from our Indian work but I was excited to go because of the opportunity to get acquainted with some of our Alliance people in that part of the country.

The camp itself was nestled in a beautiful valley in the midst of the jungle. A number of houses were built on the hills surrounding the camp.

"These homes all belong to leaders of a cult," the camp director explained. They were the only sign of civilization I could see. I had the strange sensation of being surrounded by enemies.

The first two days of ministry at the camp were extremely discouraging. The meetings lacked life and a heavy atmosphere hung over the grounds. A group of teenage girls did their best to disrupt the meetings and were having a strong negative influence on the other campers.

That night, as the other two pastors and I prayed together before going to sleep, we asked that the

Lord would somehow use us to change the spiritual atmosphere in the camp. I had in mind that perhaps He would give one of us a divinely inspired message the next day, but He had other plans.

We extinguished the Coleman lantern in our cabin and tried to get comfortable on the wooden bunk beds. The camp was bathed in thick tropical darkness and we were soon asleep.

An hour or two later I woke with the terrifying feeling that I was being attacked by an evil being hovering over me. I let out a blood-curdling scream and began flailing away with my arms, sending the wooden slats in the bed above me clattering to the floor. Fortunately the bed was empty.

The other pastors woke with a start. I quickly assured them it was only a nightmare. One of them had also at that exact moment been having a nightmare and the noise I made gave him such a scare that he thought he was going to have a heart attack.

Right next door to us was the girls' cabin. The commotion also woke them. We called through the wall assuring them that we had not been attacked by bandits and encouraged them to go back to sleep.

We tried to do the same but it was not easy. It was still pitch dark. We were nervous. We jumped with every creak and groan of the rustic cabin. Finally, after a word of prayer, we were able to doze off.

Next door things were starting to happen. First, the girls began singing choruses to calm themselves down. Then came a time of prayer and confession followed by more singing.

Before the sun had spread its warmth over the valley the atmosphere of the camp had changed. The resistance to the work of God's Spirit was gone and the campers could hardly wait for the first meeting of the day. God continued the work He had started the night before and the camp ended on a high note.

Monday morning I climbed on a bus and started the long journey back home. There was lots of time to reflect on what I had witnessed that weekend. God had used me but certainly not in a way that would leave any room for pride.

I had preached one of my most effective messages ever—an unintelligible outburst in the middle of the night.

For this I spent two years learning Spanish?

13

The Best Thing

(Arlene)

"What was the present we gave you that you liked the most?" "What is your favorite memory of something we've done together as a family?"

We were in the middle of one of those quality times that became famous with our family over the years, times when we asked and answered questions and evaluated our life together. (We once heard Kurt remark to Karla, "Oh, oh, here comes Dad with some more of those questions!")

The Lord continues to use the answer to one of those questions to bless and comfort us and to confirm that His way was and is perfect.

"What is the best, the most important, thing we ever did for you?" we asked Kurt and Karla in 1986. Kurt had just graduated from the Alliance Academy in Quito and Karla was in tenth grade.

"The best thing?" they responded almost in unison. "The best thing you ever did for us was letting us go to school in Quito!"

How could anything, I wondered, *that caused me*

such pain bring such pleasure to our children?

When Dave and I had answered God's specific call to missions we knew He was calling us to a life of sacrifice, a life of giving up what could be considered normal rights for the average person.

During the first years of our missionary service we often joked about what we had sacrificed: canned fruit and vegetables for fresh ones every day, snowy Canadian winters for spring-like weather all year round, a slow, struggling ministry for a fruitful one with more opportunities than we had time or energy for. The "sacrifice" to that point had been very pleasant indeed.

On occasion we discussed the only real sacrifice we felt we were making—separation from our friends and family back in North America. And with that always came the painful topic of the day our children would leave for boarding school in Quito.

The kids' answer to my question brought tears to my eyes as I recalled the struggle we had gone through every time we had put them on the plane and sent them off. It was only a 45-minute trip by air, only a 12-hour drive overland but it was as infinite in distance as any separation could be.

The children usually flew from Colombia to Ecuador on Aerolineas Ecuatorianas. The jets were painted colorfully at the time to represent gigantic, bizarre birds that symbolically dominated the skies.

The door appeared at the head of the monstrous bird in about the area of the mouth and as we watched our children climb the stairs to board the plane it was as if they were being swallowed and taken away by some prehistoric monster. To me, that accurately represented the monster of separation from our children.

I remembered Dave recounting his agony during his first visit to Kurt in his first year at Quito. Dave had walked the streets of the city during the night weeping and asking God why he had to be separated from his little boy. He finally came to the conclusion that this was the price God was asking of our family and it was His will for us at that time.

Memories flooded my mind as well. I recalled the day I took Kurt to the Alliance Academy in Quito for the first time. He was going into the third grade, having taken his first two years in Canada while we were home on an extended furlough. We had talked a lot about the positive aspects of the school and he had been psyched up by the good reports from his friends.

We had left Karla and Dave waving to us from the observation deck at the airport as we boarded the flight to Quito. Some of the kids with us could hardly wait to get back to school. Others were quiet, fighting back tears.

I remembered how one of the fathers had told us about his son's comments when leaving for Quito for the first time. As the father blinked back tears his son turned to him and said, "Dad, this is the happiest day of my life!"

We were greeted at the airport in Quito by an exuberant bunch of young people who had come out with the dorm parents to meet their returning buddies. We loaded up the luggage, counted the kids to make sure we had them all and drove off to the dorm.

Their excitement was contagious and we soon found ourselves caught up in the enthusiasm and exuberance of greeting dorm parents, roommates and friends from whom they had been separated over the summer months. A party atmosphere prevailed as each one was introduced to his or her new roomate and received his or her room assignments.

I settled Kurt into his room trying to make it as homey as possible, putting out the special things we had brought for that purpose—the hooked rug I had made for him, the Huckleberry Finn pictures that had already hung in his room for several years and the bedspread and books he had chosen.

He was eager to be out with the rest of the kids and during the week I was there he seemed scarcely to notice I was around. I was happy to see him making friends with his roommate, getting established in classes and generally running with the crowd of kids his age. He seemed from all appearances to be adjusting well.

I wasn't. My days were spent doing a bit of sightseeing and drinking coffee with the other mothers who had also accompanied their children to school. We baked special treats for the kids to have after school and we talked a lot, trying to encourage one another as best we could.

"Your daughter seems to be doing so well in relating to the other girls!"

"The relationship of the dorm father with the boys seems to be good . . ." and so on.

Every once in a while I would be overcome with a sense of panic. In a few days I would be leaving to go home without my eight-year-old son. How could I do that?

"My grace is sufficient for you," was the phrase that resounded in my spirit.

I also remembered something I had heard during Bible school days: "His grace only becomes operational at our moment of need."

I knew that in my own strength I couldn't leave Kurt there and return to the village of Toez high in the Andes. I spent time in prayer and reading the Word. I read and reread the story of Hannah and Samuel. God showed me once again that He requires different sacrifices from different people. He chooses what is right for us. And once again I was able to put Kurt on the altar and sense God's peace.

The day I left Kurt will go down in my memory book as one of the most difficult days of my life.

Barb Briscoe, another missionary mother, and I planned to travel back to Cali together. Our plane was leaving around noon and we had to be at the airport by 10 a.m. That gave us time to have breakfast with our boys and take them to class.

We had been counselled that it was best to say goodbye at that first hour as the children would be busy with classwork and surrounded by friends at that time.

I had explained over and over to Kurt what was happening. We had tried over the years to prepare him for this moment. All went well as we said goodbye and he walked happily into his first class.

I went back to the dorm with the other mothers to wait for the hour of departure for the airport. They were all wearing dark glasses. As I joined them my eyes, too, filled with tears and I wished I had brought dark glasses. The atmosphere was glum as we waited in silence.

Suddenly the door burst open.

"Mommy," Kurt screamed, "I don't want you to go!"

I scooped him into my arms and we wept together as we clung to each other. We prayed again and I walked him back to class.

As the plane lifted off from the Quito airport I felt as if my heart would burst and I would die of the pain. The rest of the trip was spent in numbed silence.

Dave and Karla met me at the airport. They were anxious to know how things had gone, so we found a spot in a small restaurant in Cali where I could pour out my anguish.

With a seven-hour drive back out to Toez still ahead of us we tried to eat a bit of lunch. We were so engrossed in our pain that we didn't notice a thief walk away with the suitcase I had set right beside the table.

When we realized it was gone for good it didn't even really matter. Material things seemed so totally unimportant at the time. But every time we went to Cali after that, I scanned the crowds downtown to see if I recognized any of my clothes!

How do parents deal with the pain of such a separation? By continually going back to the cross of Jesus, laying at His feet the sacrifice of our right to be together as a family and receiving from Him the grace that is sufficient for every need.

We claimed that same grace for Kurt and then for Karla when she went to Quito the following year.

Karla was so excited about going and, being a people person, adapted well to dorm life.

On her first Sunday in Quito the dorm kids were sitting in the front of the English church with some of the younger ones sitting on the steps leading to the pulpit.

A tour group of pastors and their wives from Canada were attending the service that day. One of the pastors' wives noticed a beautiful little girl sitting on the steps and thought, "Somewhere a mother's heart is breaking because of being separated from this little angel."

She covenanted to pray for that little girl—Karla—and years later told me that she had faithfully interceded for her and our family from that time on.

Our submission to the will of God for us as a family was supported and enabled through the prayers of such faithful intercessors and others who claimed us as their adopted missionary family and prayed us through those heart-breaking times.

As we have sought to honor the Lord with our obedience we have been blessed with His goodness and grace. Our relationship with our children, their character and walk with the Lord, fill our cup of blessing to overflowing.

14

I'll Go But I Won't Be Happy

(Arlene)

Our first furlough was ending and we were visiting with several other couples after the Sunday evening service.

"What are your goals for this next year?" someone asked in the middle of the conversation.

"Just to get through it," I responded rather cynically.

It was true—I was not looking forward to that year. Before coming back to Canada for furlough Dave had told the field administrative team that when we returned we would like to live in a village in the interior so we could work more effectively with the Paez Indians.

I was less than excited at the idea of spending four years in such a remote area and of learning another language. Dave, on the other hand, could hardly wait to get started.

I knew God had led Dave to make this decision and so I did not hesitate to agree to the plan. But inside I didn't want to do it. I was being obedient in body but not in spirit.

Dave found us a small adobe house to rent in Toez, a village that served as a government center for the Paez Indians who lived in the surrounding mountains.

Nine of our Paez churches could be reached from Toez in a matter of a few hours by horseback or on foot. A five-hour drive over dirt and gravel roads would get us back to Ambachico, the Indian Bible institute where we had spent our previous term.

The house needed a lot of work to make it liveable at least by my standards. The dirt floor in one of the bedrooms needed something done to it. The open windows in the walls needed glass put in them to keep out the hordes of insects and mosquitos. The door of the outdoor toilet, now covered with only a gunnysack, needed a radical change to make it functional.

The cement we used to replace the floor in the bedroom never did dry. It might have been better to keep the dirt floor. And our house became one of the few in the town with glass in the windows.

"The gringos? Oh, they live in the house with the windows!"

We also put in a septic tank and installed an indoor bathroom.

We were still getting things organized when it came time for me to take Kurt to boarding school in Quito. I went through the motions of doing everything right but inside the pain was fierce. You've just read the account.

When I returned to Toez I became more and more depressed. I detested the hours spent in language study every day. I hated the hostility we experienced when we walked through the town. We later discovered that there were several guerrilla training bases there and they suspected we were sent by the CIA to spy on them. That explained, at least in part, the resistance we felt.

It irritated me to look up and see the faces of the village children peering at me through the windows trying to discover how these foreigners lived.

On Sundays, when the villagers came and wanted to tour my little house as part of their weekend recreation, I wanted to pull the curtains, lock the door and pretend I wasn't home.

I felt as if God had determined me an unfit parent and had taken my son away. The anger and the rebellion increased, demonstrating itself in a mire of depression.

Alone one day, I was down on my hands and knees scrubbing fiercely at the mould that reappeared every few days on the damp floors. Tears were streaming down my face as I talked to God about what I felt to be His lack of love and fairness in dealing with me.

In the midst of my ranting, I heard a whistle at the door. The villagers didn't knock—they clapped, whistled or called out to indicate they were there.

Oh no, I thought to myself, *the last thing I want today is to visit with someone!*

I answered the door to find my next-door neighbor, not a believer, standing there with a bouquet of wild flowers she had picked in the mountains.

"Ah, *Doña*, I know your heart is sad because your son isn't here so I brought you these flowers."

In that instant God used that lady to minister His love to me. Flowers have always been important to me as an expression of love. That day the Lord sent them to remind me that He did love me and knew the pain of my heart. I was overwhelmed with the warmth of His care and the sense of His presence.

Unfortunately that incident didn't change my heart. I continued to sink deeper and deeper into depression. The things I expressed to Dave led him to wonder whether or not we would even be able to remain in the ministry.

He had I Corinthains 13 posted above his desk and he spent many hours there before the Lord praying for me. We didn't communicate this crisis to anyone and living off in this isolated village we were able to hide it from our colleagues.

One day I was in the bathroom hiding from the curious faces of the villagers. It was the only room in the house without windows and with a lock on the door. I spent a lot of time cocooned by those four walls nurturing my rebellion.

I picked up a book from the basketfull I kept there to help pass the time and began to leaf through it. It talked about getting over depression by praising the Lord.

Just another one of those simplistic Christian formulas that don't work, I thought to myself.

But as I continued to read, the thought came, *What have I got to lose?* I had cultivated self-pity and rebellion for so long that I no longer had the emotional energy to pull myself out by sheer determination. Why not give praise a try?

So I did. I began to make a sacrifice of praise to the Lord. And as I praised, my stubborn will began to submit to His will and I took the first steps to recovery.

In a short time I was able to genuinely praise. And, even more importantly, I learned to obey Him not only in being physically where He wanted me but in spirit as well.

Finally I was prepared to experience what we would later look back on as some of the most glorious and blessed times in our entire ministry.

15

Petrona

(Arlene)

Revivals are not supposed to begin until after the missionary arrives. But once again God was doing things His way.

We were still in the process of moving into the town of Toez when we began to get word of an extraordinary moving of God in the area. Reports from the Indians as they came down from the villages in the mountains told of reconciliations in the church, of confession of sin, of whole families coming to Christ.

The revival began when a humble Indian lady became ill. She began to have visions and then told these visions to the church leaders.

Petrona was totally uneducated, could not read or write and spoke only the Paez language. The messages she received in the visions were always a call to repentance, to reconciliation, to purification of the church.

A few weeks after arriving in Toez we were invited to a convention in the area where Petrona lived. We had attended Paez church conventions before and knew what to expect. Believers would come from as far away as two or three days' walk.

The meetings usually started on a Thursday night and ended on Sunday night. Visitors from the outlying churches would bring produce to add to the food the host church had collected from the congregation. Meals were prepared in huge pots over open fires.

Sleeping accommodations for the 200 or 300 visitors were no problem. Many ended up in the homes of the local church members. Others stretched out on their mats or ponchos on the church floor and a few even spent the night around one of the kitchen fires.

We had been invited to this convention for an official welcome into the area. After a five-hour trip on horseback up and down winding mountain trails we arrived to an effusive welcome by several hundred people waiting in the open area in front of the church.

As we slid off our horses the people lined up to shake our hands and greet us with huge smiles. A large banner hanging in front of the church expressed the message in words.

The atmosphere was exuberant and festive as we were led into the church where our lunch of *sancocho de gallina* (chicken soup) was served. There was still some time before the afternoon meeting so Dave asked if we could talk with Petrona. He had been praying that the Lord would give him discernment. He knew she was a key figure in the growing revival and he didn't want to be deceived into giving his approval to a false prophet.

Petrona was ushered into the room and offered a chair. She was a short, thin, young woman and appeared to be extremely shy. We realized we were probably the first people outside of her tribe that she had ever spoken to. Since we spoke almost no Paez and she spoke no Spanish, one of the church elders agreed to serve as an interpreter.

We questioned Petrona about her visions and were amazed at the depth of her spiritual insight. As far as we could tell there was nothing in what she said that would in any way classify her as a false prophet. It seemed impossible that this shy, illiterate woman with a baby tied to her back would be able to respond to our questions in the way she did unless the Holy Spirit had been her teacher.

A passage of Scripture kept coming to our minds: "But God chose the foolish things of the world to shame the wise; God chose the weak things of the world to shame the strong. He chose the lowly things of this world and the despised thing . . . to nullify the things that are, so that no one may boast before him" (I Corinthians 1:27-29a).

Women are not regarded as equals with men in the Paez tribe and yet Petrona was treated with great respect. Weak through sickness and lowly as an uneducated, impoverished woman, it seemed that Petrona had been chosen by God to bring a renewal to the Paez churches in the area.

We returned home after three days, amazed at the things we had seen and heard.

Our move to Toez a few weeks earlier had left us with a feeling of isolation, the impression that we were miles away from the real world. Yet in God's world we were right in the middle of the action. We went home convinced that God had other things besides language study in store for us.

Only one of the nine churches in the area could be reached by car. We had to walk or ride horseback for anywhere from one to eight hours to reach the others. However, there were a good number of believers' homes within walking distance of our village and this gave us ample opportunity for ministry while at the same time continuing with language study.

Meetings were held in different homes almost every night. The church leaders determined which places we would visit depending on whether the moon was full enough to light the way to more difficult areas or on which side of the mountains the guerrillas had been reported to be more active.

The revolutionaries in the area had decreed that the night belonged to them. The people were free to travel about anywhere during the day but exercised great caution once night fell at six p.m. Information networks kept them informed of danger.

Often a backslidden Christian under deep conviction would invite a group of Christians to have a service in his home. This would be his way of saying, "I'm ready to come back."

One Sunday our village was full of people who had come into town for the weekend. One man, obviously drunk, came up to Dave and began to talk in Paez. He was astounded to hear Dave reply in Paez. After finding out that Dave was a missionary, he told him he had been a Christian years before but now was living far from God. He invited

Dave to go to his house for a service later that week. Still drunk, he went around inviting all kinds of people in the village to the meeting.

On the designated night Dave and several believers went up the hill to his house. It was full of people but the host wasn't there. He had forgotten about the meeting!

He soon arrived, however, and authorized us to go ahead with the service. By the time the final hymn was sung tears were streaming down his face and both he and his wife recommitted their lives to the Lord.

Later that night the little band of believers that had accompanied Dave to the home made their way back down the moonlit mountain trail. Before branching off on their separate paths they stopped for a word of prayer. It was one of those special moments when the presence of the Lord is so real. Truly the Lord was at work among the Paez.

A woman who committed her life to Christ during this time of revival asked her husband, who had been attending church with her, to forgive her for things she had done in the past. He refused. One week later he fell off the cliff at the edge of the road and drowned in the river below.

This news spread like wildfire, putting the fear of God into people's hearts.

With the revival, too, came a deep desire on the part of the believers to be instructed in the Word of God. Dave and I were the ones they looked to for that instruction.

While our primary purpose in being in the area was to learn the Paez language, we realized that immediate attention needed to be given to corrective teaching. New prophets had appeared and the believers were becoming confused by their message.

One of the prophets told the people, "Don't bother bringing your Bibles to church anymore. You don't need them. God has given me some new teaching that I will pass on to you." Another stated that milk was to be used instead of grape juice when serving the Lord's supper.

Some reports we heard left us uneasy and we prayed earnestly that the church leaders would have discernment and that the true working of the Holy Spirit would not be hindered.

16

New Life at La Cruz

(David)

Most of the Paez churches had been founded years before but sin had hardened the hearts of the people. Few were following God with a whole heart and few had been attending the services in the little churches sprinkled throughout the mountains.

The Paez are a strong, independent people, proud of their history of fiercely resisting Spanish occupation of their territory. They are also masters at holding grudges and are not subtle when they have something against another.

One brother told me one day, "We are not like the whites who have hatred in their hearts yet smile and greet each other as if nothing is wrong. When we have something against another we let them know it. We don't smile and greet them on the trails or converse with them." This represented honesty and integrity to him.

The atmosphere among the Christians before God began to move was full of strife and coldness and many had stopped going to church in order to avoid contact with other brethren.

Now God's message of repentance given through Petrona and the response of the people was the chief topic of conversation throughout the entire area. People who had stopped giving their tithes and offerings began to give again as their fellowship with God was renewed.

The church buildings were in a deplorable state due to neglect and lack of funds for maintenance. New life was evident as congregations began to whitewash their buildings, clean up the yards and plant flowers.

All the churches were full to overflowing every Sunday now with crowds of people standing outside straining to hear the messages, anxious to be part of what God was doing.

The elder of one church told us that for 15 years they had a dirt floor in their church but since the revival, offerings had increased to the point where they could finally put in a tile floor—the ultimate in luxury as tiles and cement had to be purchased in a town hours away and transported by mule up the steep trails to the village.

Several weeks later I asked how work on the floor was progressing.

"We decided to use the money to help support four young evangelists," he said grinning from ear to ear. "A tile floor will be left behind when the Lord comes. Souls won to Him will not." That statement summed up the new priorities the church was setting.

The two most notable characteristics of the revival were confession of sin and the restoration of broken relationships.

I was asked to use our Jeep to pick up a dying man at the hospital an hour's drive away. He wanted to come home and get a few things straightened out before he died.

The next week the man called his family to his bedside and proceeded to confess his sins against them and ask their forgiveness. Many others came to make things right with him and, as they did, they made things right with God, too.

When the man died a week later communication in the family had been restored and many problems that had divided the church were resolved.

Our language informant asked us to pray for a Christian in his town whose life was in danger. Her husband, in a drunken rage, had tried to kill her and she had fled to the home of one of the believers for refuge. The believers protected her, rotating her from house to house in the village as her husband stormed about trying to find her, telling everyone that he was going to murder her. The believers prayed for his salvation.

On Sunday he went to the church to see if his wife would appear. He stayed to accept the Lord and he and his wife were reunited when the change in his life proved to be sincere.

One day as I rode my horse over and around the last hairpin curve on a trip up the mountain to the village of La Cruz I was met with a round of fireworks and hosts of greetings from hundreds of believers exuberantly waving flags. I felt as if I was in the midst of a gigantic political rally instead of the beginning of a weekend of preaching and teaching.

It was announced that there would be a communion service the next day. I discovered that over three years had passed since the church in La Cruz had last celebrated the Lord's Supper. The reason? The church leaders didn't want to get rid of the sin in their lives.

The Paez take seriously the admonition in I Corinthians 11 about self-examination and confession before participating in communion. Their way of avoiding the judgment associated with unworthy participation was simply to not celebrate the Lord's Supper.

That announcement initiated a time of public confession of sin such as I had never experienced. One after another the believers stood in the front of the church confessing their sin and asking forgiveness, then going to other believers and shaking their hands as they received it. Even the children participated, many of them weeping as they asked their parents to forgive them for their rebellious ways.

This confession and reconciliation went on without interruption until 3 a.m. when the lay leader terminated the meeting, announcing that it would continue in the morning. He explained to me that there was still much sin to be confessed and they would need more time before the communion service to complete their work of purification.

The next day, after the last person had confessed his sins, a glorious time of celebration began. A genuine cleansing had taken place and new life had been breathed into the congregation.

A few months later, during Easter week, La Cruz hosted one of the largest Paez church conventions that had ever been held in the area. Over 800 believers met for four days of teaching and preaching.

It was their custom to parade through nearby villages singing and announcing the meetings over a portable loudspeaker. But the religious leaders in the nearest village sent word to La Cruz that they were prohibiting any parade through their village at that time.

To avoid problems, the Christians decided to cancel the parade. Some of them still remembered the persecution they had suffered a few years earlier in that same village. One of their pastors had been placed in crude stocks and ordered to renounce his faith. When he refused he was brutally beaten and left to die. Only the loving care of the believers in the area kept him alive.

In spite of the neighboring opposition the weekend celebration marked a high point in the revival. The Paez are good organizers and the revival seemed to increase their desire to do everything in an orderly way.

During the outdoor meetings, with multitudes of people sitting on the hillsides listening to the messages, elders with long wooden sticks kept an eye on the crowd. People who conversed together or nodded off to catch a little sleep received soft taps on the shoulder to remind them that important things were being taught. Even the children paid close attention.

The river where the baptisms would take place

was about a kilometer down a narrow, winding mountain path. To avoid the confusion of 800 people making their way down the steep trail, the elders organized the crowd so that they would go down in single file. The sight of that multitude of believers strung out for almost a kilometer down the mountainside was spectacular—so spectacular that it caused a considerable stir in the village that had prohibited the parade.

That village was situated on top of the mountain on the other side of the valley from where the baptisms were to be held. Believers later told us that the religious leaders had nervously watched the proceedings during the weekend, expecting some type of reprisal for prohibiting the parade.

When the parade down to the river for the baptismal service began they assumed the believers were on their way to their village.

One of them fainted. Another kept repeating, "The evangelicals are coming. What am I going to do? The evangelicals are coming. What am I going to do?"

God was truly at work among the Paez and His enemies were starting to tremble.

17

"Taxi, Lady?"

(Arlene)

"You want a taxi, lady?" It was 2 a.m. as Karla and I sat huddled in the dark under my poncho trying to fend off the chill of the night. After unsuccessfully trying for half an hour to get a taxi to drive us up the mountain to Ambachico, I had about given up.

We had resigned ourselves to spending the night there on a wooden crate beside a food vendor's stand. The owner of the stand had long since closed up shop and gone home. And now the crossroad was deserted except for an occasional passing car.

I was afraid. No reputable person traveled these roads at night. I talked and prayed with Karla, trying to turn this nightmare into another missionary adventure so that she wouldn't be as frightened as I was.

Huddled in the darkness I recounted once again all that had happened since we had left Toez 22 hours earlier to make what normally was a four or five-hour trip.

The road from Toez to Silvia was a treacherous one and few of our trips were made without some untoward incident—a landslide, part of the road washed away, a bridge out, flat tires or any number of other mishaps that seem to take place off in the wilderness where there are no service stations or tow trucks.

The Jeep we were buying wouldn't be ready until the next week. Our Wycliffe friends, Mariana Slocum and Florence Gerdel, were nervous about us going off into the interior with the old Mission vehicle we had been using and offered to loan us their newer Wagoneer.

Now we were on our way back out to civilization to meet other missionary colleagues at the Bible institute and travel with them to our annual missionary conference another three hours from there.

We got up at 4 a.m. and loaded the car with all the things we would need at the conference: bedding, reports, our latest furlough clothes to show off in what was a kind of annual parade of missionary fashions, my needlework to do during boring business meetings and two tupperware containers of goodies to share at the coffee breaks.

The night before Dave had filled the tank with gas from the barrel we kept behind our house. He also checked the tires for air. One had to be diligent in these things. There were no service stations between Toez and the Bible institute.

We started off at 5 a.m. allowing time for the usual unexpected incident. We were to be at the Institute in time for lunch. *Six hours should be plenty,* we thought to ourselves.

Karla snuggled down in the back seat to finish her sleep while Dave and I talked about our expectations for the conference and renewing acquaintances with colleagues we hadn't seen in a year.

We were making good time over the single dirt track as the sun came up. It was a beautiful day and exotic birds and butterflies flitted across the road as we passed.

Traffic on the first part of the journey wasn't a problem. Other than the bus that made one trip daily into town there was only one other vehicle in Toez besides ours.

A bigger problem was the Indians who walked down the middle of the road, often chewing cocaine which reduced their alertness. We would come up behind them, honk and come to an almost complete stop. When startled like that in the country silence, they would freeze. Then, not knowing which way to run, they would often start off in one direction only to stop and dart back in the opposite direction. We had learned not to proceed until we knew for sure which way they were going.

The first two hours of the trip were idyllic.

Just outside of the town of Inza, which marked the halfway point of our trip, the car stopped. The motor just quit and wouldn't start again. Dave checked under the hood and came to the conclusion that the problem was beyond his mechanical abilities.

We pushed the car to the edge of the road and waited for someone to come by. The first vehicle to arrive was a bus on its way to Inza. Dave talked with the driver who told him that there was a mechanic in Inza that might be able to help. So Dave got on the bus and rode into town, leaving Karla and me with the car. We got out her books and opened one of the cookie containers and began to wile away the time.

About an hour later Dave returned with a mechanic who was obviously drunk. The whole population had been partying all weekend and everyone over 12 years of age was drunk. Dave and the mechanic worked on the car until noon and finally got it going again. Relieved, we drove into town and were able to buy lunch on credit.

There were no banks and no mail service in Toez, so each month we would calculate how much money we needed until the next trip out to the city. This time our calculations hadn't included the un-expected expenditure of paying workers to build us a septic tank. We were down to our last few cents. Actually, I had emptied the children's piggy banks into a bag before we left just in case we needed extra cash.

After lunch we thanked the Lord that the vehicle was fixed and were merrily on our way once again.

One kilometer later Dave was once again check-ing under the hood. As we sat there, several cars came from the direction we were headed and yelled something to us. We couldn't hear clearly what they were saying and just assumed that the yelling and the waving were part of the weekend festivities. We waved back.

Then a small car with three passengers drew alongside us. The driver rolled down his window and asked us where we were going.

"Silvia," we replied.

"There's been a huge landslide an hour down the road that has completely stopped traffic. There's so much mud and rock that it'll be at least three days before the road is opened again."

"Where are you heading?" Dave asked the driver.

"To Cali. We came to spend the weekend sightseeing in the area and visiting the Indian burial caves. But we have to be back in Cali to work in the morning. We're going to try to get through the back way."

We knew from past experiences that the alternate route meant an extra 12 hours on the road but Dave was concerned about Karla and me spending the night in this town with everyone drunk.

Seizing the opportunity, Dave asked the driver if he would take us with them. The Renault 4 already had three adults in it— about the comfort limit for that size of car. Add another adult and a child for a 12-hour trip over dirt roads? It was a lot to expect. Surprisingly, the driver didn't hesitate.

"Sure," he said, "but I won't be able to take any of your luggage."

I quickly grabbed my purse and poncho and a couple of small items for Karla. We crawled into the back seat.

"Wait for me at Ambachico," Dave shouted as we drove off. "I'll be out as soon as I can." Those were the last words I heard from him as we drove off.

By now it was 4 p.m., exactly 12 hours since we had gotten up to begin this "four-hour" trip.

As we drove, the conversation took its inevitable

turn to what on earth a Canadian family was doing living out in the wilderness with the Paez Indians. They talked about their concept of the Indians and their way of life and I talked about the Paez Christians I knew and how Christ had given them hope and purpose and changed their lives.

As we talked I wondered, *Could the purpose behind all these problems we've had on this trip be that I present the gospel to these people?*

Sensing the seriousness of the opportunity, I carefully explained that the message we preached and taught to the tribal people was available to them, too.

The response of this gracious couple and the blind lady accompanying them was, "*Que lindo!* (That's really nice!)"

We stopped for supper and while they went inside a roadside store to eat I bought Karla a coke and a bag of chips, using up the last of the change I had taken out of the piggy banks that morning.

Karla had become good friends with the blind lady who rode in the back seat with us. She was quite enjoying this unexpected detour.

Night fell abruptly as usual at 6 p.m. The darkness was intense—no moon, no houses with lighted windows to interrupt the inky blackness. The lights from the car seemed to end in a wall of black trees as we went around bend after bend in the road. We were alone.

Suddenly the car swerved sharply then stopped. We got out to see what had happened and found ourselves in ankle-deep mud. We were stuck.

We three ladies pushed the car through the

mudhole and emerged covered from head to toe
with mud splashed up from the spinning tires. We
hopped back into the car. It wouldn't start. With
the help of a truck driver who had come up behind us, we pushed again but the mud was so
deep that we couldn't get up enough speed for the
motor to kick in.

By this time there were three other big trucks behind us wanting to get past. Soon six men appeared.

"Let's just push the car off the road so we can get
by," one suggested. Another thought they should
all try just one more time to help get the car
started. So, while they pushed, I prayed and lo, for
the first time that day, my prayer was answered!
The car started, we hopped in and started off, care-
ful to keep in front of those trucks in case we
needed them again.

We arrived in Piendamo at 1:30 a.m. Here the
highway continued on to Cali but I needed to
travel another half hour up the mountain on
another road to the town of Silvia where the Bible
institute was located. Everything in Piendamo was
closed including the one small hotel. Nothing
would be open until 5 a.m.

The people in the car didn't want me to stay
there and invited me to go on to Cali with them
and spend the rest of the night at their house. Only
at my insistence did they leave Karla and me there
in the night by the side of the road. I watched them
drive off.

For what seemed like the hundredth time that
day I asked the Lord for protection and help.

✦ ✦ ✦

"You want a taxi, lady?"

The rough voice startled me and it took me a moment to decide. The voice was coming from a dilapitated vehicle that years ago had probably been a decent car. It didn't take me long to respond.

"Yes," I said. "How much to go to Silvia?"

We agreed on a price.

"I have to go do something first," the driver added. "I'll be back in a minute."

Karla and I were once more alone in the darkness. I didn't expect the car to return and was just resigning myself to spending the night on that cold corner when I saw the old taxi approaching.

This time there was another man in the front seat with the driver. We climbed into the back and sat down on the wooden bench that replaced the back seat.

A few minutes into the trip and I knew what the driver had been doing during the 20 minutes he had been away—he had been drinking.

I hugged Karla tightly to me as we balanced ourselves on the bench and started up the mountain. It was freezing cold. There was no glass in the windows. Both men had one arm hanging out the windows. I wondered how they could be so oblivious to the penetrating night air.

I soon realized that it was necessity that had the driver bring along a friend and it was necessity that moved them to have their arms out the windows. They were holding the doors closed! Neither door latched properly and every time we went around a curve the doors would have swung open but for the arms holding them shut. Again I prayed for safety.

What am I doing out here in the darkness with two drunk men in a dilapidated taxi? I asked myself. The idea was almost laughable.

The headlights gave off about as much light as a small flashlight as the car coughed and wheezed its way up the mountain. On the way up I prayed we'd make it to the top. On the way down I prayed the brakes wouldn't fail. I would have been moved to pray even harder if I had known the whole truth I was about to discover.

At the entrance to Silvia two policemen stopped the taxi. Traffic at this hour was most unusual and made the officials nervous. They came carefully up to the side of the taxi and asked the driver for his license. He did not have one and admitted he never had had one. In spite of it all, however, we were permitted to pass.

Finally, at 3 a.m., I knocked on the door of the Wycliffe missionaries who lived at the Bible institute and borrowed money from them to pay the taxi. The hot tea they gave us was the most delicious thing we had tasted in a long time.

I related the experiences of the day and as I talked I realized that the Lord had been in control of the entire situation. With every setback He had provided a way out.

Dave arrived the next day with his story of what had happened back in Inza. Cars left unattended on those roads were quickly stripped by thieves so he knew he had to get the vehicle off the road into some protected area. In answer to prayer he was able to get it going long enough to nurse it to a house a few yards up the road.

The lady agreed to let him park it there under her care. Dave slept in it that night. The next day he borrowed busfare from his hostess, leaving his watch and the tupperware containers of cookies with her as surety.

We arrived at the missionary conference two days late but we made it.

At the end of the conference Dave took a mechanic and the needed part back out to Inza. The car was repaired and was eventually returned to our friends.

Travel in Colombia helped us understand that although we made plans, He is the one who directed our paths—often unfamiliar ones.

18

Empty Arms

(Arlene)

The silence was breaking my heart as I sat with the Paez Indian women on the cowhides at the front of the church. I looked around me. In many ways this was like countless other services I had attended since moving to Toez.

The church was made of adobe with swept dirt floors and a zinc roof. A small table at the front, covered with a colorful tablecloth bought at the local market, served as the altar and pulpit of the church.

Many of the believers walked hours over the mountain trails to get here and would arrive at any time before, during or after the service. No matter when they came their offering was respectfully deposited at the front of the church. That offering often consisted of a bag of potatoes, a bunch of onions, one or two eggs wrapped in strips of banana leaves or a live chicken with its feet tied together to keep it from running around the sanctuary.

After the service the people would hold a believers' market, selling the offerings and thus transforming them into money to be used by the church.

The men and older children sat on the benches in the back half of the church listening to the message being given by Dave. The floor at the front of the church was usually occupied by mothers nursing their babies, toddlers wandering back and forth between aunts and other relatives, and the village dogs seeking a bit of extra warmth for their emaciated bodies and their countless fleas.

So many times the constant commotion, the restlessness of the children and the babies crying in the services had made it hard for me to concentrate, but today there was a strange silence.

Today there were only a few babies and toddlers in the church. A measles epidemic had claimed the lives of almost all the children under three years of age in that area. I wept at the sight of these mothers with empty arms, no babes sucking at their breasts.

"Are you dying?" is the Paez equivalent of "How are you today?" and is the common tribal greeting when one member of the tribe meets another on the mountain trails.

The answer is either, "No, I'm not dying," or, if the person is even a little sick, "Yes, I'm dying." The greeting reflects the general pessimism that years of suffering have woven into the character of the Paez Indian. As we lived and worked with them we came to understand this pessimism.

Due to natural isolation and poverty, medical help was not easily available and often sicknesses that could have been treated led to death. A trip to one of the small government hospitals was, in the Paez mindset, synonymous with death. I soon came to realize that any medical aid I could offer often marked the difference between life and death.

Every few years epidemics of measles and mumps accompanied the rainy season in the mountain villages where the Indians had little resistance to the white man's diseases. That lack of natural resistance along with the general malnutrition of the children and their chronic respiratory infections made them prime targets for complications such as pneumonia and meningitis.

The Colombia Department of Health regularly sent out teams to vaccinate the children but because of past experiences when already weakened children had been vaccinated, contracted the disease and died, the parents were loathe to take their children to receive the vaccine.

I bought cases of antibiotics for Cristina, a Paez believer who had taken a short course in nursing given by the local authorities, and together we vainly tried to combat the epidemics as did several other health agencies. More often than not we were contacted too late to make much of a difference.

On one occasion even Dave, who had never given an injection in his life, was called upon to help out. He was on his way to preach in a church several hours up the mountain when we received word that there was a baby there who was gravely ill with measles.

I gave Dave a crash course in giving an intramuscular injection to an infant and sent him on his way with a syringe of long-acting penicillin. We later received the happy news that the child's life had been saved—one of the few that were.

In the middle of the epidemic two things happened that caused us to recognize that our time in Toez could be cut short.

Three government officials arrived at our house one day and began to interrogate us about the measles epidemic and our participation in it. Complaints about the evangelicals had reached the ears of the government in Bogota and a commission had been sent out to investigate those complaints.

Apparently we were being accused of teaching the Indians to refuse medical aid and to resist the vaccination program in the name of religion.

I tried to explain that while we certainly did teach that God is our divine Physician, we also believed that He worked through doctors, nurses and medicine. I told them what I was doing to help and showed them my medicines. They still didn't believe me.

Then Karla, who was five years old, came in from playing with her Indian friends and greeted the visitors.

One of the officials grabbed her by the arm, rolled up her sleeve and found the scar from the smallpox vaccination she had received as an infant. I could feel the anger and the tension dissipate as she said, "Now I believe what you are saying."

In the next breath she offered me a job with the public health department there in the interior!

It was during the time of epidemic that we

turned on the radio one evening and accidently picked up a communication between the National Guard in Bogota and the local priest in Toez.

The priest had been very antagonistic towards us and had rejected any overtures of friendship and cooperation Dave had offered. The priest was calling in the National Guard to "deal with the undesireable element" in the town.

The unsettledness of our situation and the open opposition that we had faced when we moved into the village led us to exaggerate the importance of our presence in this traditional Catholic enclave. We therefore jumped to the conclusion that *we* were the "undesireable element." The National Guard obviously was coming to deal with us.

During the night as we listened to the transmission directing the soldiers through the mountains to the village we prayed and made plans for when they arrived to take us prisoner.

Imagine our embarrassment when Dave went out in the morning to see what was happening and found out that the soldiers had been called in to set up a massive vaccination program against the "undesireable element" of measles and mumps!

When the epidemic subsided we learned that almost every family had lost at least one child.

In church the chatter of the children and their undisciplined activity no longer distracted me from worship. Instead, it drove me to the Lord in tears of gratitude that at least these lives had been spared. I prayed that the Lord would soon fill with new life the empty arms of the women who sat on the floor at the front of the church.

19

Keeping a Low Profile

(Arlene)

In less than a year several hundred people had accepted the Lord, over 100 had been baptized and hundreds of believers had made new commitments to the Lord. Satan, of course, was not taking this passively.

Slander and overt hostility toward the believers produced much tension. Guerrilla activity was making travel increasingly dangerous. Evangelicals were being denied medical aid at the little outposts sprinkled throughout the mountains.

Dave was called to the Mission office in Cali to talk with the lawyer who handled the legal affairs of the Mission. The government was beginning to refuse visas to groups that had missionaries working in Indian tribes. Dave was informed that our Mission was in a precarious position because of our working in the tribe but that the government would accept our living there as long as we were in language study.

No problem! The Paez language was so difficult we knew that could be a long time!

We were instructed to "keep a low profile" to avoid drawing attention to ourselves. *How does one keep a low profile in the midst of revival?* we wondered.

Shortly after that, a church about two kilometers from Toez held special meetings during which about 20 people made decisions for Christ.

On the last day of the meetings they decided to have a baptismal service. A group of about 120 met at the church and then marched through our town carrying a portable record player playing hymns through a loudspeaker. Between hymns they announced the baptismal service and invited all who heard to join the parade.

In front of our house they stopped and held a short service, praying for us and dedicating our work to the Lord. Then they went on their noisy way once again.

Keep a low profile? Impossible!

The revival continued and, as it did, opposition increased. Government officials in Bogota sent more delegations out to investigate us. Their visits always left us uneasy and we lived under the constant threat of being expelled from the area.

I was told that because my visa stated my profession as "housewife" and not "missionary" I was prohibited from nursing, teaching or preaching.

To add to the uncertainty, we received word that Edwin Denis, one of our associate missionaries working with the Guambiano tribes, had been forced out of the town of Puente Real and relocated to the Indian Bible Institute in Silvia.

Visas for two couples waiting to get into Colombia were also being held up while the government officials worked at getting us out of the area.

Newspaper articles in *El Tiempo*, one of Colombia's leading newspapers, accused us of being spies, of growing cocaine and of causing a "war of gods" among the Indians. They could not conceive of anyone living and working among the Indians without some ulterior motive.

One afternoon, following a meeting with a government representative, our yard filled up with a delegation of Indian brethren anxious to know what was happening. We knew our time in Toez was running out and we didn't want our leaving to be a surprise to the churches.

So Dave explained to them what was happening—the reports to government authorities in Bogota, the pressure on the Mission to take us out of the area, the probability of our having to leave so that the rest of the Alliance work in Colombia could continue.

It was an emotional time both for them and for us. We will never forget the sense of God's presence and power when Cristina, who had worked with me in getting medicines out to different areas of the tribe and who had become a dear friend, spoke up.

"You are foreigners," she said, "and the government officials can make you leave. But we are Colombian citizens and they can't make us leave."

She raised her arm high over her head and looked up at the mountains.

"We will carry the banner of the gospel to our people at any cost."

It was electrifying.

A few weeks later we moved back to Ambachico. We had gone to live in Toez primarily to learn the Paez language. The Paez New Testament that was being translated by Wycliffe missionaries Mariana Slocum and Florence Gerdel was nearing completion. We looked forward to the day when we would be able to teach the people using a Bible that spoke their language.

Our proposal to the Mission had been to assign us to the tribe for a minimum of 10 years. Now, one year later, we were involved in other ministries that didn't leave time or opportunity for further language study.

Was the year of language study in Toez a waste of time? The only sense we could make out of this was that we still had many things to learn. There in Toez the Lord was able to teach us some of them.

We learned the importance of teaching the Word and discipling new believers. Both of these proved to be important factors in the survival of the church in the tumultuous days that lay ahead.

Certainly the revival did not take place because we were there and it didn't end when we left. God in His mercy and His wisdom allowed us to observe and participate in that great moving of the Spirit. We would never be the same.

We had gone out with our agenda, but God had His—not only for us, but for His Indian sons and daughters.

Some years later one of our Indian pastors told us this story.

The guerrillas were becoming more and more powerful in the area surrounding the Indian Bible Institute where we had a number of churches.

Because the guerrillas insisted that they were the "owners of the darkness" and only they and their collaborators were allowed to safely walk the trails at night, many of the churches had ceased having evening services and some had no services at all.

Since the church leaders could neither be coerced or bribed to cooperate with the revolutionaries, they became their targets. One of our pastors was killed by the guerrillas. The tension increased. Many of the church leaders lived each day with the knowledge that their name was on the guerillas' "hit list."

Due to the danger and the threats, this pastor had also closed the door of his church and the believers were holding clandestine meetings in homes. They would arrive before dark, have their services and once it was light again, would quietly sneak back down the mountain trails to their homes. It seemed the logical way to deal with the problem.

One night God spoke to the pastor: "I was the One Who called you to pastor the church. Why are you living in fear?"

The pastor realized that the God he served and Who had called him was mightier than any guerrilla force in the area.

The next day he went to the church, threw open the doors and announced that meetings would resume. That night the church was packed and many believers who had left the Lord out of fear made a new commitment to Him. Other pastors took courage from his example and soon the churches were all open again.

After two years in Silvia we were transferred to Cali. The dream of a prolonged ministry among the Paez was to remain only that—a dream. The rural phase of our ministry had ended and we would now be spending our time walking concrete trails in the jungles of urban centers.

Since that time the Paez churches have developed their own administrative structure, they are in charge of the Bible school and have shown themselves to be a mature church.

By 1984 they had planted an additional 20 congregations and in 1990 they sent their first missionaries to a neighboring tribe. Several dedicated Paez brethren have given their lives to teaching their people to read their native language and to use the Scriptures that have now been printed in Paez.

Perhaps the Lord didn't need us after all to minister to the Paez. Perhaps we needed them to teach us to walk in the midst of the moving of the Spirit of God.

All we know is that we went where He led and in His economy neither our time or our efforts were wasted.

20

A Fresh Start

(David)

It was an historic moment. Our missionaries had gathered for the annual field conference in January 1979. We were preparing to vote on a resolution that would radically change the way we were doing missions in Colombia.

We listened as the resolution was read for the last time: " . . . that all missionary personnel, except those assigned to the Bible Institute in Armenia, and some special ministries, be eventually withdrawn from their present locations and assigned to a cooperative church-planting effort, mainly in the city of Bogota." The vote that followed was unanimous.

What had led us as a Mission to this historic decision?

The Alliance had been working in Colombia for over 50 years. Some 200 churches and congregations were scattered throughout the country and our role as missionaries was primarily maintaining existing structures. The challenge of pioneer evangelism and church planting that had been so much a part of our missionary call was becoming a distant memory.

The missionaries themselves were increasingly restless. Was this all there was to missionary life or was there still an opportunity in Colombia to be involved in pioneer church planting?

A newly formed Evaluation and Projection Committee had begun wrestling with some of these questions two years earlier. Its task was to evaluate the current status of the work and to come up with a strategy for the Mission for the next few years.

As we talked together we sensed that God was about to do a new thing in Colombia. We prayed and asked for guidance.

It was one a.m. when we felt that the Lord was giving us a clear answer. A fresh start was in order! Radical changes were needed to revive that pioneer, cutting-edge spirit that had been the basis for our call to missionary service. Mission and Church were not the same thing and while we could not work independently of the National Church neither could we forget our mandate to go where others had not gone, to open up new areas for the gospel.

In subsequent planning meetings we discussed what was happening in Lima, Peru where a concentration of resources and personnel was producing some extraordinary results. Why couldn't we as a Mission focus on Bogota, the capital city of Colombia? And why not initially focus on the middle class? In spite of the fact that Colombia had a large, emerging middle class, not one of our 200 churches was making any effort to reach that unreached people group.

Excitement mounted as our missionaries thought of the opportunity of once again being involved in pioneer missions.

✦ ✦ ✦

(Arlene)

When we left the Indian Bible Institute in 1979 and Dave took up his new responsibilites as field chairman we felt as if the most exciting chapter of our ministry as missionaries had ended. After all, out there in the interior working with the tribal people we had been "real" missionaries. It could only be downhill from here on. Little did we suspect what the Lord had still waiting for us.

In the summer of 1980 we began our second furlough and once again it was extended an extra year for study purposes. I worked in the emergency department at a hospital in Regina, Saskatchewan and Dave taught a Missions course at Canadian Bible College while completing his final year at the Seminary.

During that time the Bogotá Project took its first steps.

The guest house in Cali was sold and the Mission office was moved to Bogotá. Two couples were assigned to begin the work of building bridges with the existing churches in the city and to lay the groundwork for the planting of a church in a middle-class area of North Bogotá.

We arrived in the summer of 1982. Dave's assignment would be to coordinate the Bogotá Project as

well as serve as field director. I would manage the
guest house and teach in the Bible Academies that
had been started in several of the small churches in
peripheral barrios of the city.

Seasoned missionaries joined the new ones to
form a dynamic team that in a short time would
see a church planted and growing.

One of our first responsibilities was to find a
suitable meeting place. That place turned up in a
middle-class shopping district in North Bogota.

Meetings began immediately. During the week
the entire team spent its time making contacts and
inviting people to the church. We called the church
"El Encuentro"—The Meeting Place—and installed
a bookstore just inside the entrance.

During the first month we sometimes had more
missionaries than Colombians in the services. We
had been warned that if we were going to target
the middle class we should expect no more than
three or four couples coming to the Lord in the
first year. So we were not too discouraged. But in
God's perfect timing the ministry there coincided
with growing insecurity and need in the neighborhood. People began to seek us out in their search
for inner peace and safety.

The first convert of this work was Juan Gabriel, a
young fellow who lived next door to the guest
house. He was the despair of his mother as he
wasted his time drinking and partying. At the same
time, he participated in a charismatic Catholic
youth group and deep inside wanted a different
life.

With entrance exams for the university medical

program coming up he asked one of our missionaries to pray that he would pass the exams. He did well and was accepted in the state university. This led to the opportunity for another missionary to present the gospel to him one day in the park across the street from his home.

According to his testimony later, the presentation was so forceful that he finally yielded to the Lord basically to alleviate the pressure. But he also sensed that God had met him in a special way. From that time on Juan Gabriel was a faithful member of the Bogota Encounter Church.

His sister Gloria was delivered of addiction to drugs and also became a new creature in Christ with a dramatically transformed life.

Another convert was Helena, a rigidly religious woman who was shopping in the center one day and noticed she had lost her valuable watch. She went from shop to shop asking if anyone had found it and when she stopped at our bookstore she was invited to the Sunday services.

She came the following Sunday and accepted the Lord after the service. The change in her life gave new meaning to the truth that Christ makes us new creatures.

Helena was from an upper class family and had accompanied her husband to Argentina as part of the Colombian diplomatic corps. But her life was a living hell. Rejected by her husband, an official in the military, their home was a continual verbal and sometimes physical battleground.

During one of the beatings Helena pulled out a gun and tried to kill her husband. God graciously spared her from a good aim and the bullet lodged in the floor, where it remained as a reminder to her of that temporary insanity.

She was given money to run the household and to feed her children and husband, but she herself was forced to eat in the kitchen with the maid. She did sewing and clothing repairs for neighbors and friends to earn a little money for her own basic needs. This pressure was designed to force her to leave, but Helena had nowhere to go.

Several weeks after she accepted Christ I noticed that she was actually a beautiful woman. The former bitter expression on her face had been transformed into one of peace. She was a new creation in Christ.

The change was so dramatic that her children wanted to know what had happened. Several came to church to see what El Encuentro was all about. Some of them accepted the Lord, others did not. Helena's home situation did not change but she had found love and acceptance in Christ.

By the end of six months our congregation had grown to 30.

21

Death and Life

(Arlene)

O ne Sunday, Fernando and Marta, a dynamic young couple with two children, came to the service. They had become Christians while in university and had been attending the InterVarsity meetings on campus. When they graduated they and several other couples were unable to find a church in the city where they felt comfortable in inviting their unsaved friends.

So they decided to start their own. After a few months of meeting together and studying the book of Ephesians, however, they realized they were not ready nor qualified to start a church. They felt that God was showing them they needed to become committed to an existing local church and give themselves to ministry there.

When Fernando and Marta returned the following Sunday we were ecstatic. Fernando told one of our team that they felt this was the church where God wanted them. We could hardly contain ourselves! Here was a mature Colombian Christian with experience in preaching and leading Bible studies—

a future leader for our church!

That Sunday afternoon Fernando called the leader of his university group.

"Marta and I have found our church!" he exclaimed enthusiastically.

That Sunday evening when the missionary team met for prayer we couldn't stop talking about the future that now looked more promising with the support and participation of Fernando and Marta.

Tuesday morning the phone rang early. I heard Dave say, "Oh, no!" and ask, "When?" and "What happened?"

When he hung up he could hardly speak. Fernando was dead. The funeral would be held that day in another church but because of Fernando's declaration on Sunday we were asked to participate in the service.

We were in shock. What was the Lord doing? This young man had two small children, was in the prime of his life and career and showed great potential as a church leader. Now he was dead. It seemed that our hope and faith died a bit, too.

What had happened? Fernando loved his children and when they seemed to be continually sick with colds and other illnesses the doctor had told him that his tonsils were infected and were a source of infection for his children. To remedy the situation Fernando decided to have his tonsils removed.

On the Monday following their second visit to the church he had entered the hospital to have what was supposed to be a routine tonsillectomy. Marta visited with him until about nine p.m. and then left to go home to the children. Just two hours later, at 11 p.m., she received a call. Fernando had hemorrhaged suddenly and died.

One of our missionary couples ministered to Marta and the children. We went to the funeral as a team and met many of their friends and family members. We shared their grief, weeping with the loss of this one we had just come to know but who had already won a place in our hearts.

The following week Marta expressed the desire to have a memorial service in our church. Many of their family and friends had not been able to attend Fernando's funeral because he was buried less than 24 hours after he died. (In Colombia, burial must take place quickly as embalming is not generally practiced.)

Our small chapel was packed to the doors. Among the group were about 10 professional couples from the InterVarsity group who were also looking for church homes.

The service was a triumphant one. The gospel was clearly preached and there was an atmosphere of peace and love throughout. Once again God was working out His perfect plan.

The visitors liked what they experienced that afternoon. Many of Fernando's original study group later became members of our church. Our initial board was made up almost entirely of those leaders. Two became our first Colombian pastors.

Ricardo Diaz, a 24-year-old businessman, was one of those who attended the church for the first time for Fernando's memorial service. Less than two years later Ricardo sold his insurance company to come on staff as a pastor. His wife, Gloria Estela, resigned her job as a bank manager in order to dedicate more time to the church. They both went on to seminary training at Nyack and in 1992 returned to become senior pastor of what by then had become a church of 800. Marta, Fernando's widow, became the church administrator.

God had turned death into life, defeat into victory.

"Unless a kernel of wheat falls to the ground and dies, it remains only a single seed. But if it dies, it produces many seeds" (John 12:24).

Kurt and Karla with pets at Ambachico.

The plane that crashed at Herrera.

Loading up the generator for an Indian country conference.

Petrona and her family.

Paez conference at La Cruz.

Kurt leads the trek.

Paez band . . .

. . . and coffee break. Coffee is served in large bowls.

Porfirio, on the left, was the first believer among the Paez. He eventually became an evangelist and the tribal lawyer. Marco Abel, next to him, was killed in the 1994 earthquake.

Toez — all that was visible after the 1994 earthquake was one white roof.

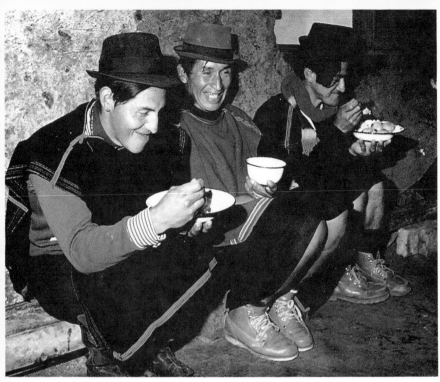

A house meeting with Guambiano Indians. Skirts are worn by the men.

Arlene chats with Guambiano women at a convention.

A leadership training session at the Ambachico Bible Institute at Silvia.

Defending the Hall of Justice in Bogota where high court officals were murdered.

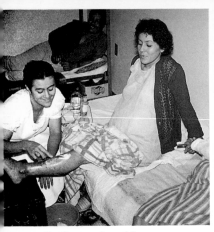
Stella, on the table, was "saved by the bull."

The human tragedy of the volcanic eruption at Armero.

A helicopter surveys the ruins of Armero.

The Bogotá Encounter Church where the walls came down.

This cross appeared in the sky during the ground-breaking ceremony for the new El Encuento Church.

Leaders at the Encuentro Church.

Arlene teaching at the Bible Institute in São Paulo.

Carnival celebration in São Paulo. The women in white represent the "Mother of the Spirits," the highest rank in spiritism.

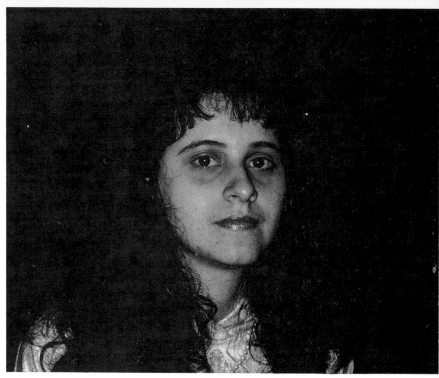

Rosana, who renounced her spiritist past to follow Christ.

This store sells artifacts for spiritist worship. The stuffed figure represents one of the major demons.

The beach at Guarujá where David Jones encountered the spiritists.

The skyline of São Paulo, the world's third largest city.

A service at São Paulo's Igreja Aliança do Aeroporto
(Airport Alliance Church); taken at the former location, below.

David with Dr. Peter Nanfelt, Vice-President of the Division
of Overseas Ministries, in the new Airport Church.

David with Jorge Motta, one of those who came into the church through
Fernando's death. Taken at the Alliance offices in São Paulo.

David and Arlene on the balcony of their São Paulo highrise apartment.

Arlene talks with a Brazilian believer.

Kurt and Karla, taken in 1986.

22

The Impossible Dream

(Arlene)

"When the trumpets sounded, the people shouted," intoned the pastor, "and at the sound of the trumpet, when the people gave a loud shout, the wall collapsed."

The pastor finished his sermon by quoting Joshua 6:20 and challenging the congregation to trust the Lord to bring down the wall separating our rented meeting place from the one next to it in the shopping center.

Since Fernando's death, the church had experienced continuous growth and we had more than filled the space. We needed a bigger place to meet and the people began to seek the Lord for direction. The atmosphere was charged with anticipation.

Everyday someone had an exciting testimony to tell of opportunities to testify, of people accepting Christ, of people finding the church. In some ways it reminded us of the revival in Toez. There, however, we had been mainly observers as God did a mighty work. Now we were given the opportunity to be participants.

Again we thought, *These are the most exciting days of our lives!*

One day I was getting ready to close up the church. I had spent the day at the bookstore taking my turn as part of the pastoral team on duty to deal with any inquiries, need for counseling or prayer, etc. We had determined that the church should be open to the public with pastoral assistance available every day. We advertised this in the literature we distributed and also announced it in church each Sunday.

This was a dramatic divergence from the usual church practice of that city where opposition and crime had led to church doors being closed except for services. The bookstore, installed just inside the front door of the church, also gave us an added reason to remain open.

The day was ending. It had been an unremarkable day. Several members of the Catholic charismatic community had visited the store. I had spent some time conversing with them, listening to their testimonies and recommending some books for them to read.

I had also worked on my Bible Academy classes for the next week. At closing time I went into the church office to gather up my things.

"Doña Arlene," I heard the clerk from the bookstore call. "There is someone here who needs to talk with you."

I went upstairs and was introduced to a young man who had just arrived at the door.

"Do you have time to talk with me?" he asked.

"What would you like to talk about?" I responded somewhat cautiously.

"I need to know God. Someone told me that here you could tell me how I can know Him. Can you help me?" he asked again.

I sensed a note of desperation in his voice.

"Yes, I can!" I responded with more enthusiasm.

I proceeded to explain the plan of salvation and when I asked him if he wanted to receive Christ as his personal Savior he didn't hesitate.

"That's what I came for," he exclaimed.

This young lawyer found new life in Christ. He represented many whom God brought to us, prepared by the Holy Spirit to receive the gift of His Son.

Prayer meetings took on a new dimension as we saw the type of problems people were wrestling with. Sometimes we were called to prayer on behalf of family members who had been kidnapped and were being held for ransom.

Other times we were asked to intercede on behalf of relatives who were involved with drug trafficking. At times we went to the Lord to pray for comfort for those left behind when a loved one had been brutally murdered either in political or drug conflicts.

No Sunday passed that we didn't have new people in the services and the church grew to the point of bursting its seams. We had been in that location only one year but with attendance crowding 100 it was time to move.

A store front two doors down from us opened up and we now had a place that would seat 200.

One year later we were full and needing to move again. Someone came up with the idea that if we knocked out the two walls between our present location and the previous one we would have seating for 300 people.

Great! Only one obstacle stood in our way. The store inbetween was occupied and the renters didn't see any reason to move.

So a time of prayer and fasting was called. "Bring down the wall," the pastor challenged. Within only a couple of weeks the renters suddenly moved out and we soon found ourselves with the space we had prayed for.

While the walls came down, the enthusiasm and the faith of the congregation soared and the church continued to grow. By the end of the third year the church was once again full. But now there were no more walls to knock down.

We had been looking for property in a casual way ever since we had moved into Bogota and had found little in that area of the city that was suitable.

A few blocks from the church there was a huge empty lot. It was located at a busy intersection with a well-known monument making it a familiar place to everyone in Bogota. We discovered that the lot was owned by the Red Cross.

We asked if it was for sale and if it was, what it would cost. We were informed that the Red Cross never sells property and that it wasn't for sale at any price.

Our team continued to dream of that lot as the site of our future church. We began to pray. We even took pictures of the lot and asked others to pray.

Time passed and we decided to look for alternatives, realizing that a choice piece of property like that would probably cost two or three million dollars even if it could be bought.

In September the administration of the shopping center we were meeting in informed us that by the next spring the entire center was to be torn down and a new one built. We had to be out and into a new meeting place by then.

It seemed an impossibility since we still had not found any suitable property. The fact that we also didn't have any money made the situation even more critical. Once again the church was driven to seek the Lord.

The dream of that lot facing the Heroes Monument had not faded for some. So we decided to ask just one more time about the possibility of buying the property.

One of our pastors went to the Red Cross office to inquire and was told, "Oh, we're not handling that property from this office any more. We just turned it over to a real estate agency."

It was for sale!

The next days were a flurry of phone calls and visits to the agency. Negotiations began. The price was set at $480,000, an incredible bargain. Bargain or not, we still didn't have more than $20,000 in the bank.

But God had forseen that need as well.

A Christian businessman, one of the men God had used in getting the Lima Encounter program

going, was in Bogota when we received word that
the Red Cross property was for sale. Within a few
days he had phoned the North American Alliance
headquarters and offered to donate $280,000 to
the project if the Alliance could come up with the
other $200,000.

A week later Dave received a call from Nyack
telling him to go ahead with the purchase of the
property. On December 24, 1985 the final contract
was signed—a wonderful Christmas present for the
church.

We later discovered that the Red Cross had
owned the property for almost 20 years but circumstances had never been quite right for them to
build on it. The city of Bogota had zoned the lot for
philanthropic or social use, prohibiting the erection
of a commercial center or a service station there. In
addition, no building higher than two stories could
be built on the back part of the property so it could
not be used for apartment blocks.

These restrictions greatly reduced the value of the
property. It was obvious that God had used all of
them to keep that piece of property for the building of the Alliance Church in Bogota.

The following Sunday we held an open-air service
on the lot to dedicate it to the Lord. The congregation was ecstatic. We marched around the property
through the long grass as if we were entering the
promised land. It was a clear sunny day with few
clouds in the sky and it seemed that in the warmth
of the sunshine we were basking in the blessing of
God.

We all joined hands in a circle before the Lord,

our hearts full of wonder at His working. The impossible dream had become a reality.

We celebrated with the traditional feast of *lechona*—whole pigs stuffed with rice and vegetables. While we were talking, eating and visiting, someone suddenly pointed to the sky and shouted, "Look!"

There, right over our property, was a cloud in the precise form of a cross! The cloud hovered over us and only began to dissipate an hour later as the celebrations came to a close.

The congregation took this as a sign of the confirmation of God on the purchase of that property and the promise of His blessing in the future.

23

Saved by the Bull

(David)

I t was one of the most amazing stories I had ever heard. Stella, six months pregnant, was quietly telling me an incredible saga of tragedy and deliverance.

Stella was only one of a small group of refugees who just two weeks earlier had survived a devastating natural disaster. In November of 1985 a volcano had erupted, melted its ice cap and deposited a three meter (10 feet) high sea of mud and lava on the city of Armero just 100 miles from Bogota. Few of the city's 23,000 inhabitants survived. The ones who did lost everything they owned.

The eruption occurred only one week after a shocking man-made disaster. A group of terrorists had occupied Colombia's Justice Palace in Bogota and in the ensuing battle with government troops 13 Supreme Court Justices had died.

Colombia was in a state of shock. The day after the volcano incident a television reporter ended his news commentary by lifting his eyes to the sky and crying out, "God! What are you trying to say to us?"

The same question crossed my mind two weeks later as I walked through, or rather on top of, Armero and witnessed the dimensions of the tragedy.

A few of the survivors were making feeble efforts to dig out some of their belongings. A thick uneasiness filled the air. Would the mountain explode again? Where would we run if it did?

Decomposing bodies had been emerging out of the drying mud during the past week. The stench was suffocating. Twenty thousand people were buried underneath us. Bodies, banks, schools, churches—all entombed in the mud and lava.

People were anxious to tell their stories, anxious for us to pray for them. And inevitably the question "why?"

One man told us how he had lost all his loved ones to the volcano. Another told of suicides he had witnessed as people realized they were the only survivors in their families.

There were also stories of divine intervention. One church finished its Wednesday night prayer meeting an hour before the volcano erupted. But the people decided to stay and pray a while longer. When the mud swept through the city an amazing thing happened. The wall of mud divided just before reaching the church, passed by on both sides and joined again on the other side. The church and those in it were untouched.

Later that week I talked with a lady I had known 15 years earlier. She was from the Ibague Church where we had spent our first year in Colombia. I had led her to the Lord and baptized her. She had married and was living in Armero.

It was a tearful reunion as she told me how God had spared their lives. Their home was in an area of the city built on a hill. As the sea of mud rose, she and her husband had climbed to the roof of their house and waited there throughout the night. The mud came to the windowtops and stopped there.

They could hear the cries of their neighbors, many of them also on their rooftops. They were able to shout words of encouragement and used the opportunity to urge their friends to turn their lives over to God. Later the next day they were rescued and taken to safety.

Now they were completely destitute, having lost home, furniture, clothes and documents. Their one request of me was that I pray they would have a child. They had been married for more than 10 years and were still childless.

I prayed and then told them half-jokingly (I certainly didn't consider it a prophecy) that in a year's time they would have a child. God answered that prayer and one year later Jonathan David was born.

God provided for this couple in another way also. Through a gift from World Relief Canada they were able to build a modest home and begin their lives again.

But back to Stella and her incredible story.

As a young person Stella had given her life to the Lord. She quickly forgot, however, her commitment to God. A house, a husband, two small children and another on the way—things seemed to be going quite well for Stella.

The last few weeks had been a little unsettling as

the long-dormant volcano became active. Local authorities assured the populace that everything was under control. There was no need to be concerned. A warning system would soon be in place that would give everyone ample time to evacuate the city if necessary.

But the volcano gave no warning. Most of the city was asleep when the first wave of mud swept through. It was almost midnight and Stella and her family were jolted awake by a dull roar that kept increasing in intensity.

In the darkness of the night Stella grabbed her two small children, tucked them under her arms and ran out into the darkness. She was immediately caught up in the river of mud that was already starting to pour through the door of her home. As she struggled to maintain her footing the children were torn from her arms. She never saw them or her husband again.

The mud was now up to her neck and Stella realized that she was only a moment away from death. Suddenly she felt something moving underneath her, holding her up. She had no idea what it was but it was alive. As her eyes became accustomed to the darkness she noticed that there, not more than three feet in front of her, was the head of a bull.

Throughout the entire night the bull struggled to keep his head above the mud while Stella struggled to stay on his back. Cries of the dying surrounded her and as daylight approached she was able to see the extent of the tragedy. The city of Armero no longer existed.

Just before noon Stella was spotted by a rescue

helicopter. As she was lifted by rope into the chopper she looked down at the bull that had saved her life. She wished he could be rescued along with her.

I was at a loss for words as Stella finished this moving story. After a moment of silence I asked Stella about her relationship with God.

"It was almost nonexistent before," she replied, "but it's strong now!"

Three months after being rescued, Stella gave birth to a healthy baby boy. He will have quite a story to tell when he grows up!

24

Leaving the Mountain

(Arlene)

There were days when I could understand the enthusiasm of Peter when he said to Jesus, "Lord, it is good for us to be here" (Matthew 17:4). I, too, wanted to build a shelter and stay up on my mountain in Bogota.

We were so happy in the ministry the Lord had given us. We were continually seeing fruit as never before. It seemed that each day was better than the last. I was teaching in the seminary and loved it. The opportunity to teach the Word, to interact with people serious about walking with the Lord and serving Him was exhilarating. I felt as if I had reached the peak of fulfillment and satisfaction in ministry.

At the same time, once the church had purchased its own property, Dave began to feel as if a chapter of our lives was coming to a close. As he looked into the future he didn't see a clear vision of our continuing involvement in Bogota. A restlessness began to take hold of his spirit.

A few weeks later, Dave and Argentine evan-

gelist, Walter Perez, crossed paths in Quito. Walter
had been part of a study commission to Brazil. He
commented to Dave that the commission was looking for an experienced missionary to move into Sao
Paulo and head up a church planting thrust in that
city. Dave's name, he said, had been mentioned as
a possible candidate.

Dave's restlessness grew.

In the spring of 1986 he made a trip to Sao Paulo
to look things over and to talk with Mission
leaders. We talked about it before he left.

"I don't mind if you go to look it over," I said,
"but I can tell you already that I'm not interested in
moving."

I loved the city of Bogota. Driving from home to
the church down the Autopista Norte (nicknamed
the "highway of death" by the Bogotanos because
of the numerous accidents on it) was always an interesting experience for me. As I looked at the city
in front of me it seemed as if it had the ever-chang-
ing face and personality of an unpredictable
woman. It was never monotonous, never boring. I
never tired of it.

The city had captivated me with her charms. Not
even the frequent sound of shots in the night, the
continuous atmosphere of insecurity or the occasional shock of exploding bombs diminished her
enchantment. During critical times for national
security when tanks surrounded the intersection in
front of the church they seemed more of a protection than a threat. Yes, the city of Bogota was
where I would build my temple if I could.

I was driving down the highway of death on a

Sunday afternoon on my way to the dedication of our new seminary library when God spoke to me.

It was the second time in my life that I had the sensation of audibly hearing His voice.

My thoughts had been full of excitement about the library, thinking about who would be there for the dedication. I thought of Fernando, the young man whose death had seeded the growth of the church and how much he would have enjoyed being there. His widow, Marta, would be there and she would be thrilled that the library was being named after Fernando. How exciting it was to work here!

Dave was in São Paulo but when he came back I would tell him that I definitely could not leave Bogotá.

As I stopped at a red light, unexpectedly the presence of God filled my little red Fiat.

"I want you to go to Brazil," He said.

It was as clear as that.

There was no other response for me there in His presence but, "Yes, Lord, I'll go to Brazil."

As I said it, I knew it was right. It was the good, perfect and acceptable will of God.

Brazil! That was the country God had laid on our hearts 16 years earlier.

A supernatural peace flooded my soul. It has never left.

✦ ✦ ✦

I felt like I was on a wild ride in an amusement park as the car jerked from one lane to another, swerving to miss potholes, dips in the pavement or slow-moving vehicles, then revving up to hit what seemed to be incredibly dangerous speeds.

I was afraid to take my eyes off the road in front of me for fear I would miss seeing the accident I was sure would take my life my first day in Sao Paulo.

A welcome committee had been at the airport to meet Karla, Dave and me that morning in July, 1987. Our whole outfit—eight bags—and seven people fit into the two cars travelling the ring road from the international airport towards the city of Sao Paulo where we would be working for the next period of our lives.

It was winter in South Brazil and the trees along the highway had all lost their leaves. I thought it was because of the terrible pollution of the city and only later realized it was because of the "cold" weather.

The buildings we passed, no matter what their size or function, all seemed to be gray and expressionless. The only character they exhibited was in the copious graffiti scrawled on any flat surface.

This has to be the ugliest city I have ever seen! I thought to myself.

It didn't take long though for us to discover charm beneath that gray exterior and to come to love the warmth of the people with whom God had called us to work.

It had been hard to leave Bogota. After 16 years of life and ministry in Colombia it was like leaving home. I smiled to myself as I recalled how God had pared down our personal accummulations.

Six years earlier during a previous furlough the

Mission in Colombia had moved from Cali to Bogota. They transferred all our goods that had been stored in the basement of the guest house in Cali. So, when we arrived in Bogota in 1982, our barrels were waiting for us at the guest house. They contained all the things we had collected during our married life.

After a year of furlough living with rented or borrowed goods I was looking foward to opening the barrels and getting my hands on "my things" once again.

We opened the first barrel. The smell almost blew us over. I picked up the pillow on the top. It shredded in my hands, scattering matted feathers all over the room. Everything was wet, mouldy, destroyed.

Mould had even eaten holes in my pressure cookers and aluminum baking pans. Mildew caused sheets and towels to shred as I tried to pick them up. Tupperware containers and lids were welded together from the moisture and would never be used again. The only items that survived were those made of glass or porcelain.

Tears threatened to spill over as we saw our books practically turned to pulp from the three or four inches of water on the bottom of almost all the barrels. Of all the things we lost, the loss of our library was what saddened us the most. The words, "The Lord giveth and the Lord taketh away" took on new significance.

Since we were to live in the Bogota guest house that was well set up with household items and linens, I didn't need all that stuff anyway. Four

years later when we left Colombia we sold everything we owned for about $1,500.

While it hadn't been hard to rid ourselves of
material things when we left Colombia we found
other things hard to leave. We left our beloved colleagues. We had learned much from those who
were seasoned church planters as we worked
together to establish the Encounter Church. We
had found comfort in their empathy when we sent
our kids to school in Quito. They understood when
we talked about the country areas where we had
worked because they had been there.

We also left behind much of our identity. It was a
revelation to see how much of who we are depends
on where we've been, what we've done and how
well we can communicate in the regional language.

Here in Brazil it was as if we had no history. Our
lives as far as anyone here was concerned started
when we landed in the airport in Sao Paulo. It
didn't matter what we had done before. We found
ourselves doing many things we had been able to
rely on others to do before.

And, of course, our communication skills were
close to zero. We had to learn another language.
Through the infinite mercy of God, Portugese is related to Spanish and so we were able to become
functional in a few months. I often mourned the
loss of the beautiful, lyrical Spanish language I had
worked hard to master.

In order to learn Portugese I had to close off the
part of my mind that operated in Spanish. While it
would be nice to speak Portugese without a
Spanish accent, secretly I'm happy that at least that

vestige of it remains with me.

We also missed our old jobs. In Sao Paulo we had to start again as learners to gain credibility both with our colleagues and those we were sent to minister to. Yes, we missed Colombia, but both Dave and I determined that we would be totally in Sao Paulo—in body, mind and spirit.

We have come to love this ugly, gray city. We have found spots of beauty and pleasure in so many places.

We love the people here—our colleagues, teammates and brethren in the church continually fill our lives with fellowship and love.

We love the Lord we serve. He took us out of a comfortable situation to put us once again on an unfamiliar path where we could not depend on ourselves, our colleagues or anything else but Him.

And we've found that middle-age doesn't mark the end of growth or usefulness as far as the Lord is concerned. I think I'll stop and write a letter to our Mission's director and recommend redeployment at least once in every missionary's career!

25

Drums and Candles

(David)

It was Wednesday night and prayer meeting was just beginning. We sat in a semi-circle and began singing the Brazilian version of "Holy, Holy, Holy."

One man in the circle had just started to attend. He had earlier given testimony to having been a spiritist priest before becoming a Christian. As we started singing he began to be a bit restless.

Suddenly he kicked off his shoes, threw his glasses across the room and leaped into the center of the circle growling loudly like an animal. The gyrations continued as he ripped open his shirt, sending the buttons flying in all directions.

Prayer took on new meaning that night as our crew of rookie missionaries joined with the Brazilians in the circle and began binding the demons and praying for the man's deliverance. For most of us this was another unfamiliar path and we were greatly relieved when the man calmed down.

I took him to the back room and continued to counsel him while the rest of the group went on with the prayer meeting.

Arriving home that night we found it hard to go to sleep. A rhythmic beating of drums, accompanied by screaming and yelling, reminded us that the spiritist center down the block was having its regular Wednesday night prayer meeting, too.

It was difficult to reconcile the sounds of spirit worship with our physical setting. The sixth floor apartment that the Mission had rented for us was located in a middle class neighborhood in Sao Paulo. Looking around us, we could have been in any large city in North America. This night, in the dark, however, it would have been easier to imagine that we were in the midst of some tribal village in Africa.

Since our arrival in Brazil a few weeks earlier we had been assailed with numerous overt signs of spiritism. A champagne glass beside a half-empty bottle of wine on a red cloth under a tree a block over from our home. The carcass of a chicken on a black cloth with some half-burnt candles and artfully arranged half-burnt matches behind our car when we came out of a church service. The "spirit houses" that adorned some yards. The green twig behind the ear of the man selling vegetables in the market. All served as constant reminders of the fact that spiritism is the most popular religion in Brazil.

The Portugese Catholics, when they colonized Brazil, had brought in a type of religion already highly contaminated by syncretism. From the Moorish Muslim invaders of North Africa, Islamic mysticism deeply influenced the Portugese. In addition, their African colonies affected the Church with its animistic world view of good and evil spirits that can be manipulated and pacified by offerings, sacrifices and ritual.

The discovery of Brazil in 1500 by Portugal found a land full of indigenous peoples who were also animistic and deeply involved in their own primitive paganism. Much later, in the 19th century, a new kind of spiritism called Kardecism, imported from France, highly influenced the religious beliefs of Brazil. Communication with the dead, reincarnation, a doctrine of "carmic works" were the essentials of this form of spiritism. They were proud of the "enlightenment" they had received from the European brand of spiritism.

When the African slaves were obligated to convert to Catholicism, it was an easy thing to assimilate the saints into their religion, giving them the same status and functions that their gods enjoyed. The names were changed but the gods were not.

The priests accepted the combining of the old worship with its dances, magic and witchcraft as long as the appearance of traditional worship was maintained.

Jesus became their god of purity; Satan, their most evil spirit. With this syncretism of the gods the people were able to hold their African-style services freely under the auspices of the church. Officially, Catholicism is the religion of Brazil, but in reality, spiritism is the religion of the people.

Iemanja, the African goddess of the sea, has come to be identified with the Virgin Mary, the queen of the heavens and the sea. Each New Year's Eve millions of people make their way to Brazil's beautiful beaches to present offerings to Iemanja.

Fresh flowers, candles and liquor are placed on miniature boats and rafts and set in the water at the stroke of midnight. If the offering is carried out to sea, Iemanja has accepted it and she will answer the prayers that have been made. If the offering returns to the beach, it has been rejected and she has looked with disfavor on the one who offered it. A bad sign.

One of our missionary colleagues, David Jones, had a confrontational meeting with the powers behind spiritism at one of these celebrations. David will tell the story.

On New Year's Eve, 1992, I was walking the darkened beach of Santa Catarina Island. My wife and I had gone there right after Christmas (Brazil's summer) for a few days of sun, surf and rest. Now, late on this New Year's Eve, I was alone on the deserted beach, reminiscing upon the year that was fast closing.

As I strolled along the sand, I came upon a circle of candles within which some carefully arranged white roses surrounded a few cigars and trinkets. I recognized it at once as a *despacho*, an offering to the spirits.

On New Year's Eve literally millions of Brazilians from all over the nation go to the beaches to bring their offerings to Iemanja, the goddess of the sea. Dressing in white, the people light candles and offer flowers, perfume, liquor and other gifts. In return they ask Iemanja and all the other spirits

they worship for their blessing and protection
throughout the ensuing year.

As I continued my walk, I saw people beginning
to arrive at the water's edge. My heart was saddened. "God," I prayed, "don't permit these lying,
demonic spirits to receive worship and honor that is
due only You. This is all of Satan and only leads to
further involvement and delusion. Don't permit this
celebration to take place here tonight. Bring a great
rain. Drown the flames of the candles and drive
these worshipers back to their homes and hotels."

As I walked, I did battle against the enemy. I
knew that other Christians throughout Brazil were
also engaged in this battle.

I watched for a few minutes as the leader of one
group of spiritists carefully arranged dozens of
candles, placing them in an intricate pattern, then
lit them, sprinkling liquor over the whole arrangement and spreading flowers at the worship site.
One of his white-clad helpers came dripping up
from the ocean where he had just made a special
offering to Iemanja. The group of people waited expectantly for one of their number to begin to
manifest a spirit. I knew that when it happened the
person would come under total demonic control,
beginning to dance and whirl like a dervish at a fantastic pace. All was set for a Satanic *festa*.

As I walked on, sickened and disgusted at what
was taking place, I continued to pray both in the
Spirit and audibly as I rebuked Satan, binding him
in Jesus' name.

It was after 11 when I returned to the apartment
where Judy and I were staying. I was still asking

God to defeat Satan and to put to shame this god-less worship.

Within just a few minutes the wind picked up, the sky clouded over and rain began to fall. How it rained! Soon the rain was coming down in sheets, whipped by gusting winds. The rain and wind extinguished the candles along the beach and sent the worshipers scuttling for protection. The wind and wind-whipped waves also made quick work of the elaborate offering to Iemanja. As I took my place with Christ in the heavenlies in warfare praying, Satan was indeed put to shame.

Brazil has passed from those times when any overt practice of spiritism was prohibited to today when spiritist centers outnumber both Catholic and evangelical churches.

Many government and business leaders regularly consult mediums and seers. Popular actors and actresses proudly proclaim on national television what brand of witchcraft they espouse. Spiritist healers perform bloodless surgery on sports celebrities.

Since arriving in Brazil we have been challenged as never before to help bring deliverance to those who are held captive by Satan.

We are convinced that this can best be done by planting strong local churches that focus on Christ our Savior, Sanctifier, Healer and Coming King.

26

Adriana

(Arlene)

" I am not going to pray anymore! Every time I pray the opposite of what I ask happens!" Alicia said quietly. "This has happened ever since we came to Sao Paulo."

As she told of the toll that the move had made on the family and especially their middle child, Adriana, I could understand why she felt that way.

Alicia's husband was an executive with a multinational company and had worked in various countries before coming to Brazil. The experience had been generally positive for the family. They were all fluent in German, Spanish, Portuguese and English.

Adriana had been a good student, doing fairly well in school in spite of suffering from petit mal epilepsy that had presented itself at the beginning of adolescence. But things had not gone well for her here in Sao Paulo. She had done extremely poorly in school.

The epilepsy had worsened and she suffered daily from multiple blackout attacks. She would study diligently for her exams and she and her mother would pray for divine enabling but when the time came to write the tests Adriana was unable to transmit what she learned onto the paper.

Needless to say this had a serious emotional impact on the family. Adriana would cry and say, "I have no future. I'll never be able to go to university!"

Things came to a crisis the day I was talking to Alicia, Adriana's mother. I had been praying for Adriana for several months and for a time there seemed to be slight improvement with better concentration and less failure in school.

Adriana was taking a strong medication—a last resort, according to her neurologist—to make her attacks of blacking out fewer. She seemed to be a little better adjusted socially and academically in school.

Then the bombshell! Adriana would have to quit taking the medicine because it was adversely affecting her liver. With that news Alicia was overcome by a sense of despair and hopelessness.

"I'm not going to pray anymore," she repeated with quiet determination.

"Okay," I said, "then I will pray until you're able to pray again."

We bowed our heads and I began to pray. I didn't really know how to pray or what to ask of the Lord but as Alicia and I entered into His presence together the Holy Spirit began to pray for us. It was an unforgettable experience in the power of prayer. Afterwards I could scarcely remember the words I had prayed because I had not formulated them, they were not mine. The Holy Spirit had been interceding for us.

The doctor took Adriana off all medication so that her liver could heal and we waited anxiously to see what would happen.

Dramatic changes became visible in all areas of her life. Her social confidence grew as her concentration improved and she saw the results in her school work.

Relationships with other young people took on new meaning and it was wonderful to see her regularly at church smiling and participating with the youth group.

A month after our prayer encounter Adriana returned to the doctor.

"You don't need medication anymore," he reported after reviewing the reports of extensive testing. The broken or nonfunctional circuits had been restored.

Adriana has not had a recurrence of the problem since then. She went on to finish high school, graduated on the honor roll and was accepted at Crown College in Minnesota—that after failing ninth grade three years in a row! A miracle of God's power and grace.

When Alicia stood before our congregation a year later and gave testimony to the power and mercy of God my heart fairly shouted, "Thank you, Lord!"

27

Rosana

(Arlene)

We had gathered together for the first meeting of our discipleship class.

"When did you receive Christ as your Savior?" I asked the woman sitting beside me.

Sonia looked at me as if I should already know. Finally she replied, "Why, when I prayed with you and Rosana two years ago!"

Her response took me back to that Wednesday night when Sonia in desperation had brought her teenage daughter, Rosana, to the church. Through circumstances no one other than the Lord could have orchestrated they had heard of our ministry.

Sonia's niece, Nicolina, a student at a university in the States, was on her way to Sao Paulo for vacation. During a stopover at an American airport she met Talita, a young Brazilian woman who had been our language teacher during our second year in Brazil. As the women conversed they discovered that both were Christians.

"If you ever need spiritual help," Talita told Nicolina, handing her our church address and phone number, "call the Alliance Church."

One Saturday night as Dave and I were finishing off a weekend seminar we noticed several new people in the front row. One was a young blonde woman who listened intently and seemed genuinely interested in what was being presented. Beside her sat an even younger woman who slumped in her seat, her head down, her long dark hair hanging over her face. I couldn't see her expression but I didn't need to. Her body language was explicit— discouragement, despair, hopelessness.

Beside her sat a young man who observed everything that was going on with an air of indifference. *I'm not a part of this. I'm just here to accompany these women,* was the message he conveyed.

As soon as we finished the seminar, the blonde (Nicolina, Sonia's niece) came up and asked, "Are you Arlene?"

When I said yes, she said, "Talita sent me to talk to you."

Arriving in Sao Paulo, Nicolina had found an untenable situation with her cousin Rosana. Rosana had been a problem child since birth, alternating between intense periods of depression and violent outbursts of rage. The family was desperate. Nicolina, a new Christian, realized at once that the problem was a spiritual one and brought Rosana to the church. The young man with them was Wagner, Rosana's boyfriend.

As I spoke with Rosana I, too, sensed a wild desperation. I asked, "Do you want to be free from this?"

Rosana started to cry as if her heart would break.

I explained that freedom would only come as she committed her life to Jesus Christ.

I asked Nicolina to return with Rosana on Wednesday night and promised that in the interim we would pray and fast for her deliverance. I wasn't sure I would ever see them again.

However, when we arrived at the church Wednesday night, three people were sitting in the church waiting for us—Nicolina, Rosana and Sonia, Rosana's mother.

Sonia told us the following story.

When she was in her seventh month of pregnancy with Rosana, her first child, a series of near catastrophes occurred. An out-of-control motorcycle crashed into their house. It destroyed a part of the house but no one inside was injured. The next day a flash flood invaded the house destroying furniture and appliances. Sonia went into premature labor. Medical intervention stopped the labor and her pregnancy went on to almost full term.

Rosana's delivery was a prolonged, difficult one but she was an apparently normal infant—normal, except that she cried constantly. There was only one room in the house where she experienced periods of quietness and rest.

Three months of caring for a screaming infant, with the doctors unable to diagnose the problem or prescribe help, brought Sonia, a fairly devout Catholic, to the point of being ready to accept advice or help from any quarter.

A relative began to take her and the baby to a spiritist center. There the medium told Sonia that someone had cursed her pregnancy and the baby.

That "someone" was a woman who wanted Sonia's husband.

When the woman was unable to get him, she had gone to a spiritist center and had had a curse put on the family. This had occurred during the seventh month of Sonia's pregnancy.

The medium also advised Sonia to attend a party. At that party, the medium said, a woman would come to her and ask her how Rosana was. That person would be the source of the curse.

It happened exactly as the medium described, giving Sonia confidence to accept the counsel the medium would now give her. For a while the situation did improve.

But the relief was short-lived. Despair and desperation returned. Rosana was inconsolable. Her fits of crying would last until she lost consciousness. Her sleep was continually interrupted with what appeared to be terrifying nightmares.

Sonia regularly visited the spiritist center and attended services there. Every Tuesday she faithfully went to mass at the Catholic Church, lit thirteen candles and prayed for peace in her home.

In her anxious search for answers she took 15-month-old Rosana to a child psychiatrist. As she sat in the waiting room the young male receptionist called her over.

"Your baby's problem isn't psychiatric," he said. "It's spiritual."

With that he offered to call a medium he knew, assuring Sonia that the medium had the power to cure the problem. Sonia consented, willing by this time to try anything.

The medium told Sonia to prepare a blend of herbs with water and give it to the baby to drink for three days. That would cure her of the crying spells.

When Sonia finally got in to see the psychiatrist and pour out her story, he also prescribed medicine to calm the baby.

Armed with these two cures Sonia decided to try them both. She sent her husband to the drugstore for the medicine and, at the same time, she prepared the potion that had been prescribed by the medium.

Rosana drank the herbal water without resistance. Sonia's confidence in the potion grew and was confirmed when her husband returned from the drugstore with the drug the psychiatrist had ordered. As he crossed the threshold of the house the bottle flew out of his hand and broke on the floor.

Three days later, just as the medium had predicted, the incessant crying stopped. In gratitude Sonia took Rosana weekly to the spiritist meetings. The baby seemed to enjoy the services, cooing and playing happily during the time they were there.

From the very beginning the mediums agreed that Rosana had a receptive spirit and one day would be a spiritual guide for others.

Life at home appeared normal at last. Twins were born. They did not evidence any of the turmoil that Rosana had experienced and brought to the family. A calm settled over the household.

That calm was abruptly broken when Rosana reached the age of 11. The periods of deep depression and inconsolable weeping reappeared for no apparent reason and persisted until she was 15.

At that time, during one of the weekly visits to the spiritist center, the medium told them that the problem was being caused by a benevolent spirit who wanted to come into her life and possess her. Only when it did, said the medium, could it bring about the desired change in her. So at that same meeting they did everything according to the ritual prescribed for Rosana to receive the benevolent spirit.

But there was great resistance in Rosana and the spirit was not able to possess her. The mediums stepped up their efforts to have her incorporate the spirit and became frustrated when the spirit "came down" and possessed the person who stood beside Rosana.

Sonia was instructed to make a peace offering—a bottle of champagne and a red rose—to the spirit to avoid unpleasant reprisals for its rejection.

As she left the spiritist center with Rosana, Sonia felt a sense of disillusionment.

This nonsense doesn't work for us, she thought as she determined not to make the peace offering nor to return to the spiritist center. From now on, she decided, she would rely on the God her traditional religion taught. She began to recite the Lord's prayer and Ave Marias whenever a crisis arose.

But, once again, no relief came. The terror at night, the crying spells and the violent rages increased until they provoked the crisis that brought the group to our church.

As Dave and I talked with them on that Wednesday night we sensed in Rosana a readiness to make a complete commitment to Christ. We read some Scripture and Dave presented the simple plan of salvation.

"That's exactly what I want in my life!" Rosana exclaimed.

As we prayed with her, Sonia, too, repeated the prayer of acceptance of Christ. It seemed too easy and I confess I was so engrossed in dealing with Rosana's problem that I didn't take Sonia's commitment seriously at that time. I assumed it was just one more item on her list of attempts to help Rosana.

Once Rosana had received Christ we had a basis for asking for total liberation from any spirit other than the Holy Spirit in her life. She renounced all that had been done and believed in the past and once again completely turned her life over to Christ.

She told us how for years the spirits had tried to inhabit her and how she constantly rejected them. It was their persistence and insistence that had caused the depressions and rages.

Dave asked her, "Why didn't you just give in to them so you could have peace?"

"Because they demanded more than I wanted to give," she replied.

"Christ wants to control your life completely," Dave assured her. "Are you willing to let Him do that?"

"That's different," she exclaimed. "Yes, I do want to give my life to Him."

The change in Rosana in those few moments was dramatic. She had come into the counseling session with a closed expression on her face and a deadness in her eyes. Now, as we finished praying, she looked up at us with a smile. There was a new light in her eyes. She had been born again. She had been brought into freedom in Christ.

That was Wednesday.

On Saturday she brought her boyfriend, Wagner, to the young peoples' meeting.

"Whatever you did for Rosana," he told Dave, "I want you to do for me. She is a new person!" That night he also prayed to accept the Lord.

Rosana grew quickly in the Lord and brought many of her family to Christ, including her brother and sister. Wagner's spiritual life fluctuated between hot and cold. When he narrowly escaped being killed on his street a few months later he made a new commitment to Christ. The bullet that missed him by a hair had brought him to a quick and fresh repentance.

The street life of drugs and bars eventually exerted an influence too strong for Wagner to resist. A year later he was shot and killed by one of his enemies.

Rosana grew rapidly in the Lord and received a call to serve Him full time. Her life continually radiates the grace of God to those around her.

I was thrilled when Sonia came to me and asked me to disciple her. As I meet with her each week I am blessed with her commitment to Christ and the wisdom she has received from the Lord since her conversion.

When we left the revival among the Paez Indians we felt that we wouldn't ever experience such glory and satisfaction in ministry again.

When we left Bogota I felt as if ministry would be kind of downhill after all that we had experienced there.

But that's not the way the Lord works. Every day is a new day, a different day. Here in Brazil we have found a new dimension of ministry that is equally, if not more, satisfying as we declare that Christ came to seek and to save those that are lost—and to set the captives free!

28

It's Not Over Yet

(Arlene)

It was one of the worst classes I had taught at our Alliance Bible School in Sao Paulo. The atmosphere was heavy.

Studying for the lesson had been a battle. I had difficulty finding good resource material. I was frustrated by the dearth of theological books in Portugese compared with Spanish or English.

I had difficulty organizing the notes I did have and I had problems understanding and finding the direction I needed to lead the students in discovery of truths that would mark and change their lives. I wasn't satisfied with what I had put together for the three-hour class on Christology.

As we prayed to begin the class there was a deadness in our prayers as if they were mere form and ritual—just a convenient, traditional way to launch into the study.

I couldn't seem to capture the interest of the students and every minute was a struggle to keep them awake and responding.

I found myself in a terrible confusion of languages with my thoughts sluggishly trying to penetrate through heavy clouds in my mind. Did I say that in English? Is that a Portugese or a Spanish word? Did I use all three languages in that last sentence? Is that word feminine or masculine?

And so the class went. I would start to present a theme and in the middle of it I would forget the major point I had intended to emphasize. Neither could I find it in my notes. I pushed on through the three hours with an overwhelming sense of failure and defeat that was confirmed when one of the sharpest students commented, "I feel like my brain is paralyzed!"

In the following days I realized that all of this had been a manifestation of spiritual opposition to the truths of the power and work of Christ that were being presented. So I decided to enlist prayer support from students and colleagues for future sessions.

The next week the class was so different, with freedom of the Spirit evident in attitudes, participation and communication. I left that class sensing that we had had a glimpse of the power and glory of Christ.

On the way home we stopped at a red light a few blocks from our apartment. Suddenly and without warning a huge man appeared in the middle of our lane.

He began to walk towards us slowly and purposefully with an incredibly malevolent expression on his face. His shoulders were raised and in his hands he carried what appeared to be a weapon of some sort.

The thought passed through my mind that the weapon was a chain and that he was going to attack our car with it. Robberies at stoplights are common in Sao Paulo.

He continued his advance, all the while maintaining his fixed, evil stare. A few meters in front of the car he raised his right arm and threw the object in his right hand to the ground. He repeated the gesture with the object in his left hand. It was as if he was throwing down the gauntlet and challenging us to a duel.

He continued to stand in our lane like the Incredible Hulk, shoulders raised, feet apart, gaze fixed, ready to attack. The light turned green and traffic began to move in the lane beside us. We, however, were prisoners, unable to advance.

Then just as suddenly as he had appeared, the man stepped to the side of the road. As we drove past the place he had been standing we saw that the objects he had thrown to the ground were small green branches that had no doubt been given special powers by the spiritists.

We felt as if we had been in a confrontation with the "strong man" who had come to deliver a message: "You won one battle tonight but the war isn't over yet."

No, it's not over yet. There will be many more battles to fight before our work and that of the Mission is finished here in Brazil.

Active involvement in missions means that one is constantly invading Satan's territory. The unfamiliar paths that must be walked are sometimes dark and dangerous. Were it not for the fact that

Christ's command to the Church is to invade enemy territory we would be fools to even try to confront the powers of darkness.

The fact is, however, that not only has Christ given the command to go, but He has also promised His presence on a 24-hour basis to those who obey His command.

And He has promised victory.

✦   ✦   ✦

How about you?

Why not get involved in missions?

Take the plunge.

Break out of your comfort zone and head down some unfamiliar path.

Of one thing you can be sure—Christ has already passed that way.

He will be your Guide.

"I will lead the blind by ways they have not known, along unfamiliar paths I will guide them"
(Isaiah 42:16).

Epilogue

We had planned for this epilogue to be, among other things, an encouraging report on the growth of our Paez and Guambiano churches.

However, the earthquake of June, 1994 that devastated southern Colombia has changed all that. This epilogue now becomes almost a eulogy and certainly an urgent call to prayer for our Indian brothers who have faced and will continue to face immense suffering as they seek to rebuild homes, churches and culture.

"Avalanche caused by earthquake kills at least 64 in Colombia."

As I started to read the article in a Brazilian newspaper I was shocked to discover that the town of Toez was mentioned. The little town that most people in Colombia have not even heard of was now being cited in a Brazilian newspaper. According to the news report, Toez no longer existed. The avalanche had completely buried it.

Our minds immediately went back to the year we lived there. What had happened to our neighbors? What about the children Karla used to play with? What about our pastors, their people, their churches?

Later that day scenes of the disaster flashed on

the TV news as helicopters flew over the area as-
sessing the damage. All that was left of Toez was
the roof of the school a half block from where we
lived. The rest of the area was covered with tons of
mud and debris that had settled into a smooth
shroud.

Over the next few days the true dimensions of
the tragedy began to take shape. More than 1,000
people killed, thousands homeless—all in the area
where we had worked during our first two terms in
Colombia.

A fax received as a preliminary report from the
Colombia field director on June 20, 1994 provided
more numbing statistics:

- eight Paez Indian Alliance pastors dead
- 29 communities affected, 27 of which had
  Alliance churches
- 25 churches completely destroyed
- 4,500 evangelical Christians (primarily
  Christian and Missionary Alliance) affected;
- 12 evangelical schools destroyed
- four teachers dead
- at least two Guambiano churches destroyed.

Fearing further landslides, the government
evacuated 2,000 Indians from the area.

Unfamiliar paths are not unique to missionaries.
The Paez tribe is confronting a major upheaval that
has obliterated many of its cultural guideposts and
is thrusting its people into territory and experiences
that are foreign to them.

Will you pray that the revival that once was

sparked by the quiet voice of Petrona will be
fanned back into flame by the devastating blast of
an earthquake and that God would use our Paez
believers to carry the message of the gospel to new
areas as He did with the Christians in the book of
Acts?

✦   ✦   ✦

A final word.

Many of you have had an important part in our
ministry through prayer and faithful giving. We
thank you.

The years have gone by. We are a few pounds
overweight and our hair is turning gray. Our
children are grown and give us immense pleasure
in their right choices and their love for God.

God has honored and answered your prayers.

And we continue to walk unfamiliar paths.

✦   ✦   ✦

Kurt Peters graduated from Toccoa Falls College
in 1993 and is an accredited missionary candidate
with The Christian and Missionary Alliance. He
lives in Calgary, Alberta, Canada.

Karla finished her nursing education in 1994. She
is married to Mel Eby and they reside on a ranch
near Prince George, British Columbia, Canada.

DATE DUE
